1 CAPITALIZATION

Take the trouble to capitalize words only according to standard principles. Do not capitalize words unnecessarily.

The rules of capitalization are generally clear and less subject to exceptions than most rules of language. Nevertheless, if you encounter problems, a good recent dictionary should help you, especially where the capitalization of a word depends upon its use: "the bible of show business" but "the Holy Bible," "my big brother" but "your Big Brother in Washington."

1A Proper names

Note that common nouns like *boulevard, heights, university, park*, and *store* are capitalized when they accompany proper nouns.

1. Names of persons or specific entities or trademarks

   Sarah Kaltgrad, J. P. Morgan, Mohammed, Nissan Maxima, William the Conqueror, the Constitution, English 101, Peabody Award, the Statue of Liberty, Cheerios

2. Geographical names

   Little Neck, New York, the Southwest, Colorado, Niagara Falls, Quebec, Rocky Mountains, Yellowstone Park, MacArthur Park, Zuma Beach, Coney Island, Germany, Europe, Asia, Missouri River, Bermuda Triangle, Rodeo Drive, Cape Fear

3. Specific nations, cultures, ethnic groups, and languages

   Mexican, Thai, Cherokee, English, Afro-American, Pacific Islanders, Tahitians, Chinese, Koreans, Bosnians, Iranians

   Farsi, English, Russian, Armenian, Spanish, Chinese, Swedish

4. Schools, institutions, government divisions and agencies, companies

   United Way, Library of Congress, UCLA, Securities and Exchange Commission, Houston Oilers, General Mills, Kent School, Red Cross, Rotary Club, Medicare, Coast Guard

5. Days, months, commemorative days, or holidays

   Monday, March, Veterans' Day, Father's Day, Thanksgiving

6. Significant events or periods, historical documents

   the Fourteenth Amendment, Middle Ages, Operation Desert Storm, the Bill of Rights, the Great Depression, Prohibition, the Constitution

7. Religious references to documents, holidays, personages or deities

   the Bible, Koran, Upanishads, Genesis, Revelations, Easter, Allah, Messiah, Christian, Hindu, Moslem, Judaic, Mormon, Christmas, Yom Kippur

8. Words used

   We all kno

   Only the al   Money remains as a motivation.

1B Abbreviations and acronyms

Capitalize abbreviations or shortened forms of capitalized words

   USC, NBC, IBM, AT&T, CA, NYC, NFL, MADD, UNESCO

1C Capitalize titles indicating rank or relationship

Capitalize titles and words denoting family relationships that precede the name but not those that follow it.

   Mama McCaslin; Cousin Jenny; President William Clinton; George Bush, the president of the United States; Governor Pete Wilson; General Taylor; George West, the captain; Phillip Stein, our governor; Aunt Adrienne; Adrienne, my aunt

When words indicating family relationships are substituted for proper names, they are usually capitalized:

   Well, Father, you certainly did well on the course today!

1D Capitalize the first word and all other important words in titles

Articles (*the, a, an*), coordinating conjunctions (*and, but, for, or, yet*), prepositions (*in, to, for, around, up, under*), and the *to* in infinitives are not normally capitalized, unless they are the first word in the title.

1E Always capitalize the first word in a sentence and the first word in directly quoted speech

   Never have so many viewers tuned in to one program.

   Are you sure? Well, then, let's cancel the wedding. I'm serious.

   Father Mike often says, "Blessed are those who are funny."

   Without hesitation, Elizabeth shouted, "Down with the Bruins!"

Keep in mind this handy rule: common (uncapitalized) nouns are often preceded by articles (*a, an, the*) or by limiting words like *each, many, several, every, some*.

1F Capitalization review chart

Capitals	No Capitals
Lieutenant Cameron Winston	the lieutenant in charge, every lieutenant
the Korean War	the gas wars of the 70's
German, Swedish, Tagalog	foreign languages
East-West University	your local university
the U.S. Army	a rough and ready army

CAPITALIZATION REVIEW CHART (continued)

Capitals	No Capitals
March, St. Patrick's Day	spring, holiday
the Midwest, Midwesterners	to fly west, midwestern states
the Retail Merchants Association	an association for merchants
Tay-Sachs disease	cancer, colds, pneumonia
a Himalayan, Toyota trucks	cats, small trucks
several Republican hopefuls	democratic movements
our Declaration of Independence	the women's declaration of independence

2 THE COMMA

Among its many functions, the comma is used to set off independent clauses, items in a series, coordinate adjectives, parenthetical expressions, and nonrestrictive phrases or clauses.

2A Use a comma to separate independent clauses joined by a coordinating conjunction (*and, but, for, or, nor,* or *yet*)

EXAMPLES:

He wanted to be a salesman, but no jobs were available.

The people refused to send their children to school, and the school building stood empty the entire year.

Be sure you understand that this rule applies to the joining of *independent clauses*, that is, complete sentences. The use of the coordinating conjunction to join compound subjects (*Bush* and *Dukakis* debated on Thanksgiving Day), pairs of phrases (The food at that restaurant is prepared *without care* and *without taste*), compound verbs (Phil *ran* the office and *acted* as athletic director), or the like does not include a comma.

2B Use commas to separate items in a series

EXAMPLES:

Friendly, small, and innovative are adjectives that accurately characterize this college.

He went to the basement, set the trap, and returned to the kitchen to wait.

2C Use a comma to separate coordinate adjectives modifying the same noun

EXAMPLES:

He washed his new, black, shiny pickup.

Himalayan cats have long, silky, heavy fur.

To test whether adjectives are coordinate, reverse their order or insert *and* between them. If the phrase still makes sense, they are coordinate adjectives and require a comma. The first example makes sense using either

method: *shiny, black, new pickup,* or *new and shiny and black pickup*.

Non-coordinate adjectives have a special relationship with the nouns they modify. To some degree, they create a word group that itself is modified. They should not be preceded by commas.

EXAMPLE:

They all admired the tall, powerful football player.

In this sentence, *football* is a non-coordinate adjective, different from the coordinate adjectives *tall* and *powerful*. You cannot put *and* between *powerful* and *football* nor can you move the word *football*. Other examples of non-coordinate adjectives are *doll* house, *art* museum, *computer* science, and *wheat* bread.

2D Use a comma to set off an introductory phrase or clause from the main clause

PARTICIPIAL PHRASE:

Having spent his last penny, Luster tried to borrow a quarter from his boss.

PREPOSITIONAL PHRASE:

At the beginning of each game, a noted singer gives his rendition of "The Star-Spangled Banner."

ADVERBIAL CLAUSE:

When the composer was finished with the prelude, she began work on the first movement.

2E Use a pair of commas to set off nonrestrictive (amplifying or explanatory) phrases and clauses inserted into a sentence

EXAMPLES:

Mary Jennings, who was my best friend, dropped the class.

The first offer on the Blake house, which had been on the market for almost a month, was very disappointing.

My son, a soldier in the 82nd Airborne Division, spends most of his time at Fort Bragg, N.C.

Be sure to distinguish between these nonrestrictive interrupters and the restrictive modifiers, which are not set off by commas. Nonrestrictive modifiers add information but do not limit or change the meaning of the sentence. Note how the meaning changes when the clause is restrictive.

RESTRICTIVE:

The young woman who was my best student dropped the class.

The young woman is now identified as the best student. Here is another example of a restrictive clause.

EXAMPLE:

Cardiac patients who have artificial valve implants are required to take anticoagulants for the rest of their lives.

2F Use a comma to set off nonrestrictive phrases and clauses that follow the main clause

EXAMPLES:

Jessica wanted to see the ice show, not the circus.

Few fans thought the reigning heavyweight champion could win, although he was superior to the challenger in every category.

2G Use commas to set off an appositive

An appositive is a noun or noun phrase that renames or explains the noun it follows.

EXAMPLE:

The novel, a mystery about a secret island off the Washington coast, was an instant bestseller.

2H Use commas to set off words in direct address

Words in direct address identify the one being spoken to.

EXAMPLE:

Excuse me, Beth, but aren't you late for your tennis lesson?

2I A comma can take the place of an omitted word or phrase

EXAMPLE:

The Capitol Bank is located in a shopping mall; the Investors Bank, in the heart of town.

2J A comma is sometimes needed for clarity

EXAMPLES:

Ever since, we have taken the plane rather than the train.

In May, Marcia went to Washington, D.C.

2K Incorrect use of the comma

Do not use a comma between a subject and a verb.

EXAMPLES:

Faulty: The returning fishermen, received a warmer welcome than they expected.

Revised: The returning fishermen received a warmer welcome than they expected.

Do not use a comma after a conjunction. The coordinating conjunctions (*and, but, for, or, yet*) and the subordinating conjunctions (*although, because, until,* and so on) are not followed by commas.

INCORRECT:

People are fully aware of sexual harassment issues today, and, they walk a straighter line.

REVISED:

People are fully aware of sexual harassment issues today, and they walk a straighter line.

Do not use a comma to set off restrictive elements. Commas do not set off a restrictive element, which limits the meaning it refers to.

INCORRECT:

My company gives great bonuses to employees, who work hard.

REVISED:

My company gives great bonuses to employees who work hard.

3 THE SEMICOLON

The semicolon is generally used to separate coordinate elements in a sentence, that is, items of the same grammatical nature. Most often, it is used between related ideas that require punctuation weaker than a period, but stronger than a comma. In addition, the semicolon divides three or more items in a series when the items themselves contain commas.

3A Use a semicolon between related independent clauses not joined by a coordinating conjunction

EXAMPLES:

A mature male gorilla may be six feet tall and weigh 400 pounds or more; his enormous arms can span eight feet.

New York has twelve major stadiums; Los Angeles has fifteen.

3B Use a semicolon between independent clauses joined by a conjunctive adverb

Frequently, two independent clauses are joined, not by a coordinating conjunction, but by a transitional word (conjunctive adverb) introducing the second clause. A semicolon must be used between the clauses because these transitional words (such as *accordingly, also, consequently, finally, furthermore, however, indeed, meanwhile, nevertheless, similarly, still, therefore, thus,* and the like) are *not* connecting words.

EXAMPLE:

A female coyote will not bear pups if her diet consists of fewer than fifty rodents a week; thus, Mother Nature achieves a population balance.

3C Use a semicolon to separate coordinate clauses (joined by a coordinating conjunction) if the clauses themselves have several commas

EXAMPLE:

The warranty on the car covered extensive repairs to the electrical system, front end, transmission, fuel injection system, and valves; but the amount of time and inconvenience involved in returning each time to the dealer cannot be ignored.

3D Use a semicolon to separate items in a series when the items themselves contain internal punctuation

Normally, three or more items in a series are set off by commas; however, when they are made more complex by commas and other punctuation, they are separated by semicolons.

EXAMPLE:

The trio was composed of a cellist named Grosz, who had been a European virtuoso for many years; a pianist who had won a major music festival in 1954, 1955, and 1958; and a violinist who had studied in Budapest, Vienna, and Munich.

4 THE COLON, HYPHEN, AND APOSTROPHE

4A Colon

The colon is a signal that something is to follow: a rephrased statement, a list or series, or a formal quotation. Use a colon in a sentence if you can logically insert *namely* after it.

Use a colon at the end of a complete statement to show anticipation—that is, to show that amplifying details follow, such as a list, a series of items, a formal quotation, or an explanation.

EXAMPLES:

Of all the gauges in an airplane cockpit, three are crucial: the altimeter, the gas gauge, and the crash-warning indicator.

After five minutes of silence, the actor uttered those famous words: "To be or not to be; that is the question."

A popover has four common ingredients: flour, milk, salt, and butter.

Problems that occur in the use of the colon usually result from lapses in the following rules:

1. Only a complete statement (independent clause) should precede the colon.

INCORRECT:

Tasks that I must complete today: mow the lawn, read two chapters of history, and tidy my room.

CORRECT:

I must complete several tasks today: mow the lawn, read two chapters of history, and tidy my room.

2. A colon should not separate essential parts of a sentence.

INCORRECT:

In updating my computer, I added: a hard disk, a laser printer, and a fine-resolution monitor. (The colon separates the verb from its direct objects.)

CORRECT:

In updating my computer, I added some new components: a hard disk, a laser printer, and a fine-resolution monitor.

ALSO CORRECT:

In updating my computer, I added a hard disk, a laser printer, and a fine-resolution monitor.

3. There should not be more than one colon in a sentence.

INCORRECT:

The success of the action depended upon three variables: that the weather would hold out, that the supplies would arrive on time, and that the enemy would be short on three things: planes, ammunition, and food.

CORRECT:

The success of the action depended upon three variables: that the weather would hold out, that the supplies would arrive on time, and that the enemy would be short on planes, ammunition, and food.

4B Hyphen

The hyphen has two main uses: to divide syllables at the end of a line and to link words in certain combinations. It is also used in compound numbers from twenty-one to ninety-nine.

Hyphenate a compound adjective (an adjective made up of two or more words) when it precedes the noun it modifies. The hyphen is ordinarily not used when the words follow the noun.

EXAMPLES:

She wore a well-used raincoat.

BUT

Her raincoat was well used.

The past-due bill lay unnoticed behind the couch.

BUT

The bill, past due, lay unnoticed behind the couch.

NOTE:

A compound adjective with an adverbial *-ly* modifier is never hyphenated: the *poorly designed* interchange. When the *-ly* modifier is an adjective, a hyphen is properly used: a *friendly-looking* dog.

4C Apostrophe

In addition to indicating possession, the apostrophe is used to take the place of omitted numbers (class of '87) and omitted letters or words in contractions (wasn't [was not], o'clock [of the clock]), and sometimes to indicate plurals (A's, I.D.'s).

Use an apostrophe to show the possessive case of nouns and indefinite pronouns.

1. The possessive case of singular nouns (either common or proper) is indicated by adding an apostrophe and an *s*.

EXAMPLES:

George's speech, the senator's campaign, anyone's opinion, the boss's office, Charles's book, Burns's poems, Dickens's novels.

2. The possessive case of plural nouns ending in *s* is formed by adding only the apostrophe.

EXAMPLES:

the girls' softball team, the waitresses' union, the Harrisons' antique cars, the Weisses' party, the Joneses' cabin.

NOTE:

Irregular plurals, such as *men* or *children*, form the possessive by adding an apostrophe and an *s:* men's, children's.

4D Incorrect use of the apostrophe

1. With plural nouns

   With very few exceptions, a writer forms the plural of a noun by adding *-s* or *-es* (gloves, galoshes, Williamses, ideas, Franklins, hot dogs). Do not incorrectly add an apostrophe to form the plural.

INCORRECT:

The numerous cat's in the neighborhood kept us awake all night.

REVISED:

The numerous cats in the neighborhood kept us awake all night.

INCORRECT:

The Williams' and Smiths' were carpooling.

REVISED:

The Williams and the Smiths were carpooling.

2. With singular verbs

   Verbs in the third person, present tense used with *he, she, it,* and other subjects always end in *-s* and never take an apostrophe.

INCORRECT:

The chairperson run's the council with an iron hand.

REVISED:

The chairperson runs the council with an iron hand.

INCORRECT:

She walk's with a cane.

REVISED:

She walks with a cane.

A common error is to confuse possessive pronouns and contractions, particularly its and it's (meaning *it is*), their and they're (*they are*), and whose and who's (*who is*). Possessive pronouns have no apostrophe. See Pronouns, section 13.

5 THE DASH, QUESTION MARK, AND EXCLAMATION POINT

5A Dash

The main function of the dash, like the parentheses, is to enclose information within a sentence. Dashes are generally more forceful and therefore should be used sparingly, since they highlight the ideas and items they enclose.

Use dashes to indicate hesitation, or a sudden break in thought or sentence structure, or to set off appositives and other explanatory or parenthetical elements. The dash adds emphasis to any part of a sentence that can be separated from the rest of the sentence.

EXAMPLE:

The skydiver—in spite of his broken leg—set a new record for endurance.

Some specific uses of the dash follow:

1. To interrupt continuity of prose

EXAMPLE:

"I really can't tolerate—Well, never mind."

2. To emphasize appositives

EXAMPLE:

The items she had asked for in the new car—tape deck, mileage computer, stick shift—were all included.

3. To set off phrases or clauses containing commas

When a modifier itself contains commas, dashes can make its boundaries clear.

EXAMPLE:

General Motors—which has manufactured tanks, cannons, and mobile cranes—has always been far more than an automobile assembler.

4. To set off parenthetical elements

EXAMPLE:

The child was sitting—actually sprawling—at his desk.

5B Question mark

A question mark indicates the end of a direct question. A question mark in parentheses signals doubt or uncertainty about a fact such as a date or a number.

Use a question mark after a direct question.

EXAMPLES:

When are we going to eat?
Ask yourself, what are the odds of winning?
(It is also correct to capitalize the word *what*.)

A question mark in parentheses may be used to express doubt.

EXAMPLE:

The Dean's notes, published in 1774 (?), are considered the novel's origin.

NOTE:

The use of the question mark as a mark of irony or sarcasm is not usually considered proper: The superintendent's important (?) announcements took all morning.

Rules regarding the use of the question mark are unlikely to cause you trouble. Problems mainly occur (a) because of failure to distinguish between *direct* and *indirect* questions (an *indirect* question is always followed by a period: My friend asked why I didn't have my car.) or (b) because of mistaken combination of question marks with other punctuation marks. A question mark should never be combined with a comma, period, exclamation point, or other question mark. Most often, the question mark assumes the functions of other marks.

5C Exclamation point

An exclamation point is an indicator of strong emotional feelings, such as anger, joy, shock, surprise, or fear. It may also be used to express irony or emphasis. Like the dash, it should be used sparingly.

Use an exclamation point after a command, an interjection, an exclamation, or some other expression of strong emotion.

COMMAND:

Stop!

INTERJECTION:

Wow! Fire! Help!

EMOTIONAL EXPRESSION:

Don't tell me you did it again! How wonderful!

An exclamation point should not be used with commas, periods, other exclamation points, or question marks.

6 QUOTATION MARKS, PARENTHESES, AND ITALICS

6A Quotation marks

One of the main uses of quotation marks is to signal the exact words of a writer or speaker. Quotation marks are also used to enclose the titles of short literary or musical works (articles, short stories or poems, songs), as well as words used in a special way.

EXAMPLE:

"Ozymandias" by Percy Bysshe Shelley is an example of an Italian sonnet.

Enclose direct quotations in quotation marks.

EXAMPLE:

"We will wage war wherever it takes us," Winston Churchill pledged.

Quotation marks should enclose only the exact words of the person quoted.

EXAMPLE:

Winston Churchill pledged that "we will wage war wherever it takes us." (NOT...pledged "that we will...")

NOTE:

When a quoted sentence is interrupted by a phrase such as *he said* or *she replied*, two pairs of quotation marks must be used, one for each part of the quotation. The first word of the second part of the quoted material should not be capitalized unless it is a proper noun or the pronoun *I*.

EXAMPLE:

"There are two sorts of contests between men," John Locke argued, "one managed by law, the other by force."

NOTE:

When a quotation is a structural part of the sentence, it begins with a lowercase letter, even though the original quotation is a separate sentence beginning with a capital.

EXAMPLE:

F.D.R. told a worried nation that "there is nothing to fear but fear itself."

However, when the quotation is not structurally integrated with the rest of the sentence, the initial letter is capitalized.

EXAMPLE:

F.D.R.'s sage words of wisdom, "There is nothing to fear but fear itself," soothed a worried nation.

Commas and periods *always* belong *inside* quotation marks; semicolons and colons, outside. Question marks and exclamation points are placed inside the quotation marks when they are part of the quotation; otherwise they are placed outside.

EXAMPLE:

What did he mean when he said, "I know the answer already"?

"The case is closed!" the attorney exclaimed.

6B Parentheses

Parentheses, like dashes, are used to set off words of explanation and other secondary supporting details—figures, data, examples—that are not really part of the main sentence or paragraph. Parentheses are less emphatic than dashes and should be reserved for ideas that have no essential connection with the rest of the sentence.

Use parentheses to enclose an explanatory or parenthetical element that is not closely connected with the rest of the sentence,

EXAMPLE:

> The speech that she gave on Sunday (under extremely difficult circumstances, it should be noted) was her best.

If the parenthetical item is an independent sentence that stands alone, capitalize the first word and place a period inside the end parenthesis. If it is a complete sentence within another complete sentence, do not begin it with a capital letter or end it with a period. A question mark or exclamation point that is part of the parenthetical element should be placed inside the parenthesis.

EXAMPLES:

> On Easter, I always think of the hot cross buns I used to buy for two cents apiece. (At the time, the year was 1939, and I was three years old.)

> A speech decrying the lack of basic skills on campuses today was given by Congressman Jones (he was the man who once proposed having no entrance standards for community college students).

> The absurd placement of the child-care center (fifteen feet from a classroom building!) was amateur architecture at its worst.

6C Italics/underlining

Italic type is the slanted type used for titles and special emphasis (*Moby Dick*). In handwritten or typed text, italics are indicated with underlining (Moby Dick).

Use italics to designate or draw attention to:

1. Titles of complete or independent works, such as books, periodicals, newspapers, plays, films, television programs, long poems (long enough to be published as separate works), long musical compositions, albums, paintings, and statues. Do not underline the title at the head of a term or research paper.

Books

William Faulkner's *The Sound and the Fury*
John Grisham's *The Firm*
Jonathan Kozol's *Illiterate America*

Periodicals

Psychology Today
U.S. News and World Report

Newspapers

The *Los Angeles Times*
The *Daily News*

(Note that the word *the* is not considered a part of a newspaper's or magazine's title and is normally not capitalized or italicized.)

Plays, films, television programs

William Shakespeare's *The Merchant of Venice* (play)
Eugene O'Neill's *Beyond the Horizon* (play)
Beauty and the Beast (film)
Fatal Attraction (film)
Molly Brown (television program)
All in the Family (television program)
A Chorus Line (musical)
South Pacific (musical)

Long poems

Sir Walter Scott's *The Lady of the Lake*
Lord Byron's *Childe Harold's Pilgrimage*

Paintings, Statues, Other Works of Art

Grant Wood's *American Gothic*
Michelangelo's *David*

2. Ships, trains, airplanes, spacecraft

Capitalize type or model names of vessels and vehicles (like Tristar or DC-10); however, italicize only those names that delineate specific craft.

Ships

The Queen Mary
The Bismarck
The Nautilus

Trains

Super Chief
Orient Express

Airplanes

The Spirit of St. Louis
The Flyer

Spacecraft

Sputnik
Apollo I

3. Words used in a special sense

Foreign words and phrases

He sadly said his *au revoirs*.

The culprit was the common dog flea (*Ctenocephalus canis*).

Use your dictionary to be sure that the word or phrase is not considered so common that it is standard in American usage, and thus not italicized: et cetera, a.m., pizza, tableau, cabaret, chop suey.

Words given special emphasis or words, letters, or figures singled out for discussion

Because of his background, his *w's* sounded like *v's*.

She calls everybody *honey*.

My English professor mentioned my overuse of the word *basically* in my writing.

Any overuse of italics for emphasis causes it to be less noticeable and therefore less effective. Use it sparingly.

---

7 SPELLING, WORD PARTS

7A Spelling

An important habit to develop, if you are troubled to any extent with spelling errors, is to look more closely at spelling in your own writing. Declare war on misspelled words: keep a personal list of words that you have misspelled. Notice that writers misspell words in three fundamental ways:

1. They misspell words they also mispronounce:

   -leaving out a letter, as in "enviorment" or "drasticly." (Correct: *environment; drastically*)

   -adding an additional syllable, as in "irregardless" or "athelete." (Correct: *regardless; athlete*)

   -scrambling sounds, as in "sangwich" or "irrevelent." (Correct: *sandwich; irrelevant*)

If you are misspelling words because of mispronunciation, look up each word you have any doubts about in the dictionary and take the time to learn the correct pronunciation and spelling. Make a personal list of words in this problem category.

2. They confuse meanings or choose the wrong word:

   -*there\their\they're; effect\affect; coarse\course* are examples of homonyms that can be confused.

   -*allusion\illusion; allude\elude; device\devise; counsel\council* are examples of words often confused because the writer is not sure of their meaning.

If you have trouble distinguishing words that have the same sound or nearly the same sound, learn those words. Use your dictionary, and keep a list of homonyms and similar-sounding words that you need to remember.

3. They do not depend upon the spelling rules for help because they have not memorized them.

Learn the spelling rules. They really do help; for most people, they are lifelong companions.

RULE #1: Words with *ie* or *ei*

There is probably not a writer of English alive today who has not depended at some time on the following old rhyme:

> Use *i* before *e*
> Except after *c*
> Or when sounded like *a*
> As in *neighbor* or *weigh.*

This rule applies only to words in which the ei/ie combination is within one syllable, not to words in which the letters are split between two syllables, such as *science* or *deity*. Other exceptions are:

ancient	Fahrenheit	caffeine	protein	counterfeit
either	neither	leisure	seize	weird

RULE #2: Adding prefixes

A **prefix** is a verbal element added to the beginning of a word or root to add to or change its form or meaning (*mono-, pre-, dis-, trans-, sub-, anti-*). A **suffix** is an element added to the end of a word or root to form related words (*-ment, -ship, -able, -ist, -ism, -ify*). A **root** is the base or core of a word, the part that contains its basic meaning, such as dis*agree*able or over*rate*d. See Word Parts at end of this section.

When you add a prefix such as *pre-* or *un-* to a root or base word such as *paid*, simply attach prefix and root together without any changes to either one, as in *prepaid* and *unpaid*.

Base words, such as *paid*, can stand alone; *roots* require the addition of a prefix or suffix before they become words, an example being the root *-cess* in *incessant*.

If the prefix ends with the same letter that begins the root, include both letters, as in *misspell, disservice,* and *illegal*.

RULE #3: Final e

A large number of words end in silent e, such as *time* and *recite*. Remember that the *e* is not pronounced. The rule has two parts:

1. When you add a suffix that begins with a vowel, such as

   -en, -ize, -ess, -ism, -able, -ible, -ic, -ist, -ance, -age, -ing, -ed, you **drop** the final e.

EXAMPLE:

word	+	suffix	=	new word
write	+	-er	=	writer
amuse	+	-ing	=	amusing
hope	+	-ing	=	hoping

2. When you add a suffix that begins with a consonant, such as

   -ward, -ment, -ry, -ship, -ful, -ness, you **retain** the final e.

EXAMPLE:

word	+	suffix	=	new word
force	+	-ful	=	forceful
life	+	-like	=	lifelike
excite	+	-ment	=	excitement

As with all rules, the *Final e* rule has exceptions. Here are a few important ones:

argument	convention	duly
intervention	judgment	truly

RULE #4: *y to i*

For words ending in consonant plus *y*, change the *y* to *i* when you add a suffix: *bounty + -ful = bountiful* and *silly + -er = sillier*. Here are examples:

word	+	suffix	=	new word
penny	+	-less	=	penniless
defy	+	-ed	=	defied
carry	+	-age	=	carriage
angry	+	-ly	=	angrily

Exceptions:

Do not change the *y* when you add *-ing* (*drying, carrying, playing*), or when the original word ends in a vowel plus *y* (rather than a consonant plus *y*): (*joyous, employment, playful*).

RULE #5: Forming plurals

1. Adding *-s*

Most words are made plural by adding *-s* to the singular form:

> pencil—pencils, home—homes, Eberle Wilson—the Wilsons, breakfast—breakfasts

2. Adding *-es*

To form the plural of words ending in *s, ch, sh, x,* or *z,* add *-es.*

> Jones—Joneses, class—classes, wax—waxes, starch—starches, church—churches

If a word ends in *o* preceded by a consonant, form the plural by adding *-es* to the singular form:

> hero—heroes, veto—vetoes, tomato—tomatoes

If a word ends in *o* preceded by a vowel, form the plural by adding *-s* to the singular form:

> zoo—zoos, patio—patios, igloo—igloos, curio—curios

3. Words ending in *f* or *fe*

For most words ending in *f* or *fe,* form the plural by adding *-s* to the singular:

> waif—waifs, proof—proofs, fife—fifes, chief—chiefs, gulf—gulfs, sheriff—sheriffs, staff—staffs

For still another small group of words ending in *f* or *fe,* change the *f* to a *v* and add *-s* or *-es:*

> calf—calves, knife—knives, leaf—leaves, half— halves, self—selves, wife—wives, shelf—shelves

4. Words ending in *y*

Form the plural of a noun ending in *y* and preceded by a consonant by changing the *y* to *i* and adding *-es:*

> berry—berries, energy—energies, theory— theories, huckleberry—huckleberries, sky—skies

When the *y* is preceded by a vowel, form the plural by adding *-s.*

> play—plays, delay—delays, birthday—birthdays, galley—galleys, alloy—alloys, tray—trays

5. The plural of proper nouns

Form the plural of names and proper nouns simply by adding *-s* or *-es:*

> Mary Jones—the Joneses, Henry—Henrys, Brooks Williams—the Williamses, Ian Wolf—the Wolfs

6. Irregular plurals

Some nouns do not add *-s* or *-es* at all to form their plurals:

> foot—feet, ox—oxen, goose—geese, man—men, child—children, datum—data, mouse—mice, basis—bases, phenomenon—phenomena, index—indices (or indexes), hypothesis— hypotheses

Others do not change at all when used in the plural:

> sheep, deer, moose, corps, cattle, Japanese, Chinese, Portuguese, trout

7. Plurals of compound words

Form the plural of a compound noun written without a hyphen by changing the last word in the combination to its correct plural form:

> baseball—baseballs, strawberry—strawberries, doghouse—doghouses, grandchild— grandchildren, somebody—somebodies

Form the plural of a compound noun made up of a noun plus a modifier by changing the most important word to its correct plural form:

> brother-in-law—brothers-in-law, commander-in- chief—commanders-in-chief, notary public— notaries public, bill of sale—bills of sale, rule of thumb—rules of thumb

7B Word parts

Recognition of word parts is one of the best ways to learn to spell correctly. It is possible to divide most words in the English language into word parts: **roots, prefixes,** and **suffixes.** Roots are remnants of words that have been derived from more than 100 languages over the centuries—languages like Latin, Middle English, Danish, Dutch, German, Italian, Spanish, and Flemish that form the basis of our language. Typical roots are **port** (carry), **dict** (say), and **miss** (send). Prefixes are word parts placed at the beginning of words that add to or qualify their meaning. Typical prefixes are **trans** (across), **pre** (before), and **inter** (between). Suffixes are placed at the end of words; while they may add meaning, mostly they indicate how the words are used in sentences. Typical suffixes are **ity** (quality of), **ness** (degree of), and **ify** (cause to become).

Roots

Root	Meaning	Example
-duc- (-duct-)	take, lead	conduct
-mit- (-miss-)	send	transmit
base-	step, base	basement
audi-	to hear	audience
psych-	soul	psyche
-scrib-, -script-	to write	inscribe
-graph-	to write	graphic
geo-	earth	geography
-tract- (-trac-)	draw	attract
-vers- (-vert-)	turn	revert, diversion
-tang- (-tact-)	touch	tangent, tactile
-path-	feeling	pathetic
-spec- (-spic-)	look	spectacle
acus-	needle	acute, acumen
therm-	heat	thermometer
manu-	hand	manufacture
-luc-	light	lucid
vid (vis)	see	vision
-dict- (-dic-)	say, tell	dictator
-gress-	go	transgression
audi-	to hear	audiometer
auto-	self	autobiography
phil-	to love	philately
-cept- (-capt-)	take	accept
-port-	carry	transportation

quad-	four	quadrangle
quin-	five	quintet
sex-	six	sextuplets
sept-	seven	septuple
oct-	eight	octopus
non-	nine	nonagon
deca-	ten	decade
cent-	hundred	century
milli-	thousand	millimeter

Prefixes

Prefix	Meaning	Example
trans-	across	transport
ante-	before	antecedent
anti-	against	antibiotic
counter	opposite to	counterfeit
post-	after	postpartum
in-	not	indecent
neo-	new	neophyte
non-	not	nonentity
omni-	all	omnipotent
super-	over	superintendent
circum-	around	circumnavigate
semi-	half	semiconscious
uni-	one	united
bi-	two	binocular
tri-	three	triple

Suffixes

Noun-Forming Suffixes	Meaning	Example
-ery	(quality of)	misery
-ence, -ance	(state or quality of)	reference, acquaintance
-al	(process of)	betrayal
-ant	(one who)	defendant
-er, -or	(one who)	miner, minor
-ion	(process of)	attention
-age	(condition, rank, service)	marriage
-dom	(place, state, condition)	freedom
-ist	(one who)	specialist
-ism	(act, practice of)	terrorism
-ate	(cause to become)	cultivate
-en	(cause to become)	strengthen

Adjective-Forming Suffixes	Meaning	Example
-al	(of, relating to)	annual
-less	(cause to become)	childless
-ant	(cause to become)	pleasant
-ible	(capable of)	credible
-ial	(capable of)	presidential
-ive	(capable of)	adoptive
-ish	(capable of)	selfish

Verb-Forming Suffixes	Meaning	Example
-ate	(cause to become)	generate
-en	(cause to become)	harden
-ize	(cause to become)	nationalize
-ify	(cause to become)	liquefy

BASIC SPELLING LIST

absence	annual	breathe	conscience	disastrous
accidentally	answer	brilliant	conscientious	discipline
accommodate	apartment	bureau	consciousness	dissatisfied
accompanying	apology	buried	convenient	dormitory
accomplish	apparent	business	course	eighth
accustom	appearance	calendar	courteous	eligible
achievement	approaching	candidate	criticism	embarrass
acknowledge	arctic	career	criticize	enthusiastic
across	argument	carrying	curiosity	environment
address	ascend	certain	dealt	equipped
a lot	association	changeable	definite	especially
all right	athlete	changing	desirable	exaggerated
always	attendance	characteristic	despair	excellent
almost	audience	clothes	desperate	existence
although	bachelor	coming	dictionary	experience
altogether	balance	committee	different	explanation
amateur	before	comparison	dining	extraordinary
among	beginning	competition	disagree	extremely
amount	believe	conceive	disappear	familiar
analyze	benefited	conferred	disappoint	fascinating
20	40	60	80	100

BASIC SPELLING LIST

February	intelligent	occurred	psychology	stretch
foreign	interesting	occurrence	quantity	studying
formerly	itself	original	quiet	succeed
forty	knowledge	paid	quite	surprise
fourth	laboratory	parallel	really	temperature
friend	led	particularly	receive	thorough
generally	lightning	pastime	recommend	till
genius	literature	perform	referred	together
government	loneliness	perhaps	relieve	tragedy
grammar	loose	piece	religious	truly
guidance	lose	pleasant	restaurant	Tuesday
handle	mathematics	possible	rhythm	unnecessarily
height	meant	preferred	schedule	until
humorous	minute	prejudice	separate	usually
imagination	mischievous	principal	sergeant	weather
immediately	necessary	principle	severely	whether
indefinitely	ninth	privilege	sophomore	wholly
independent	noticeable	probably	speech	woman
inevitable	nowadays	proceed	stopped	writing
infinite	occasionally	professor	strength	written
120	140	160	180	200

8 ABBREVIATIONS, NUMBERS

The use of abbreviations and digits has generally been considered acceptable in informal or colloquial writing, and much less acceptable in formal or scholarly writing. In fact, the more formal or elevated writing becomes, the less acceptable are abbreviations, acronyms, digits, or shortened forms of any sort. Such a rule can be overly applied, to the point that writing becomes tedious and more laborious to read. Here are some rules of thumb that might help:

• In the same way that a writer should never use a pronoun without being sure that the reader knows the noun it refers to, a writer should never use an abbreviation or acronym without being sure that its meaning is clear to the reader.

• If the use of a shortened form is customary, such as the use of digits in *May 15, 1993*, or *1447 Wilshire Boulevard*, avoid the longer form.

• The use of abbreviations and numbers is often a matter of style, and can be appropriate in some contexts and not acceptable in others. In business, advertising, and journalism, shortened forms are very popular, because they allow the writers to communicate quickly and efficiently. In school work, writing is more formal and prescribed. (*The MLA Style Manual* and *The Chicago Manual of Style* are the leading sources of information about academic conventions in the humanities, the *Publication Manual of the American Psychological Association* in the social sciences, and the *CBE Style Manual* in the sciences.)

8A Abbreviations

1. Abbreviations of titles with proper names and of words used with dates or numerals are appropriate in both formal and informal writing.

Titles before Name	Titles after Name
Dr. William Westmoreland	Willard C. Fenton, Ph.D.
Rev. William Wightman	David Sawin, M.D.
Mr. Joseph Verdi	Harriet Murray, D.D.
Gen. Norman Schwarzkopf	Howard Hardesty, Sr.
Ms. Adrienne Wilson	Edmund G. Lear, Esq.

Use abbreviations like *Dr.*, *Sen.*, *Rev.*, *Hon.*, *Prof.*, and *Rep.* only when they are written before a proper name; otherwise, spell them out.

INCORRECT:

The *Sen.* is visiting the student council tomorrow.

REVISED:

The senator is visiting the student council tomorrow.

CORRECT:

Most students at Danbury College voted for Sen. Miller.

In the same manner, *B.C., A.D., A.M., P.M., no.,* and *$* can only be used with specific dates or numerals:

77 B.C.; A.D. 1248; 4:45 A.M. (or a.m.); 11:00 P.M. (or p.m.); No. 45 (or no. 45); $5.50

(Note that *B.C.* [*"before Christ"*] always follows the year while *A.D.* [*"anno Domini"* or *"year of the Lord"*] precedes the year.)

INCORRECT:

Can you remember the No. of the batter who hit that home run yesterday in the p.m.?

REVISED:

Can you remember the number of the batter who hit that home run yesterday afternoon?

CORRECT:

It was No. 44 who hit the home run at 5:50 p.m.

2. In general, avoid the use of Latin abbreviations except in documentation of sources.

Even the common use of etc. (*et cetera*, "and so forth"), e.g. (*exempli gratia*, "for example"), and i.e. (*id est*, "that is") is less clear than the straightforward English equivalent. *Etc.* is overused; it has little meaning unless the reader clearly and immediately understands the extension of ideas or examples it suggests.

CLEAR:

Grains and nuts—wheat, corn, peanuts, etc.—are good sources of Vitamin E.

(Few readers would have any difficulty mentally cataloguing some other grains and nuts.)

UNCLEAR:

When we finally reached the ancient hotel, we toured, listened to lectures, etc.

(Most readers would have no clear idea of what other activities belong on this list.)

3. Initial abbreviations and acronyms (MIT, UCLA, UNICEF, NRA, AIDS, ACT) are acceptable in most college writing as long as you are sure your writers will understand them.

If you feel an acronym may be unfamiliar, you should spell it out at first, using the acronym in parentheses. Then you can use the abbreviation in confidence.

CORRECT:

The Fund for Instructional Improvement (FII) has supported many innovative teaching projects in California. FII grants, in fact, helped to begin the development of distance learning.

8B Numbers

1. Spell out numbers that can be expressed in one or two words. Use digits for numbers of more than two words.

CORRECT:

More than ninety people contributed to the memorial fund.

CORRECT:

He said he would die if she refused him, and, seventy-eight years later, he did.

CORRECT:

The White House has 230 regular staff members.

CORRECT:

The fact that she had 350 horsepower under her hood did not seem to please her.

NOTE:

A hyphenated number between twenty-one and ninety-nine is considered one word.

CORRECT:

A Maserati costs only eighty-two thousand dollars.

2. If a number occurs at the beginning of a sentence, it must be spelled out, regardless of how many words it contains.

INCORRECT:

235 killer whales were spotted in the Santa Cruz Straits.

CORRECTED:

Two hundred thirty-five killer whales were spotted in the Santa Cruz Straits.

BETTER:

Observers have spotted 235 killer whales in the Santa Cruz Straits.

Numbers Normally Written in Digit Form	
Addresses:	40 Pine Lane; 1 Fifth Avenue
Time:	6:15 A.M.; 9:00 P.M.
Dates:	May 26, 1993; 18 February, 1983; A.D. 1208
Exact change:	$5.75
Percentages:	66 percent; 100 percent
Fractions:	1/2; 3/8; 16/16
Divisions within books or plays:	Chapter 3; Act 2, scene 2
Measurements:	2 by 4; 13 by 10
Identification numbers:	1-700-433-0858 Ru501-6697

9 THE PARTS OF SPEECH: AN OVERVIEW

Parts of speech are the word categories of the English language, divided according to form and function within a sentence. Every word in every sentence is one of the eight parts of speech, that is, it performs one of the functions described by the parts of speech, *naming, asserting action or being, modifying, connecting,* or *emoting.* Understanding the parts of speech is a good first step in learning to employ language with confidence and accuracy.

9A Naming words

Nouns

A noun is a word that names a person, place, thing, or idea. The first words that babies speak are probably nouns. Speakers and writers use nouns to relate to the world around them and to their ideas about the world. The best way to identify a noun in a sentence is to look for the answer to the question "What?"

Persons	Places	Things	Ideas
engineer	house	meadow	honor
mother	room	tree	love
crowd	New York	spoon	ability

For more details about nouns, see section 10.

Pronouns

A pronoun is a word that takes the place of a noun. One uses pronouns to refer to persons, places, things, or ideas without naming them, a process which is usually necessary for economy of expression. The noun (or other pronoun) that the pronoun replaces is called the *antecedent.*

> Reggie built a shed. He did it for under $100.

In the sentence above, the noun **Reggie** is the antecedent of the pronoun **he**. Often, antecedents are not stated within sentences.

> Will **you** give **me** your name and phone number?

For more details about pronouns, see section 13.

9B Asserting action or being: Verbs

A verb is a word that asserts an action or state of being. There are three kinds of verbs: action verbs, linking verbs, and auxiliary verbs. **Action verbs** describe the *behavior* or *action* of the subject; **linking verbs** tell what the subject *is, was,* or *will be;* **auxiliary verbs** combine with main verbs to create a verb phrase. A clear way to identify a verb in a sentence is to change the tense or time of the sentence; the verb will usually change its form in some way.

1. INTRANSITIVE VERBS (express an action that does not have a receiver)

> Lowell **smiled** broadly.

> Elizabeth **sang** loudly.

2. TRANSITIVE VERBS (need a direct object or receiver of the action to complete their meaning)

> Herbie **bought** a new bat.

> Mary **read** a book.

3. LINKING VERBS (also called state-of-being or copulative verbs, modify the subject by associating it with a predicate noun or adjective)

> (*am, seems, looks, sounds, tastes, appears, turns, feels, grows, remains, proves* and others)

> Elfriede **looks** unhappy.

> Latisha **remained** president of the stamp club.

4. AUXILIARY VERBS

> (Forms of *am, have, do;* also *will, would, can, could, may, might, have to, ought to, need to, dare to* and others)

> The team **is** coming here on December 17.

> Charlotte **will be** sent home if she wears those shorts again.

> UCLA **will have** won for the third time.

For more details about verbs, see section 11.

9C Words that modify or describe or limit

Adjectives

An adjective is a word that modifies, describes, limits, or, in some other way, makes a noun or pronoun more clear and exact. Adjectives can be identified by noting that they answer these questions: *Which? What kind?* or *How many?*

Adjectives are the least movable of modifiers within a sentence. Usually they occur before the noun they modify; a descriptive adjective can also appear as a predicate adjective after a linking verb (as in "The cat is *enigmatic*").

Types of Adjectives:

DESCRIPTIVE:

> the *nasty* editorial, the *beautiful* sentiment, the *warm* living room

ARTICLES:

> *the, a,* and *an*

PROPER ADJECTIVES:

> *German, Mexican, Western, European, Christian, English*

COMPARATIVES:

> *hard, harder, hardest; careful, more careful, most careful*

POSSESSIVE:

> *my, her, your, its, our, their*

DEMONSTRATIVE:

> *these* magazines, *that* house, *this* route

INDEFINITE:

some food, *either* car, *few* students, *any* shoes

INTERROGATIVE:

Whose rules? *which* rooms? *what* crime?

NUMERICAL:

the *forty-second* President, the *third* revision, the *fifth* time

For more details about adjectives, see section 12B.

Adverbs

An adverb is a word that modifies a verb by answering the questions *how, when, where,* or *why* about the action the verb is performing.

The bear ran *heavily.*
The corps *sharply* turned to the right and *smartly* saluted.

Adverbs can also modify adjectives or other adverbs, usually by means of words that indicate degree or intensity.

She wore an *exceedingly* formal gown.
They prepared the meal *very* hastily.

Adverbs are quite movable within a sentence, and work effectively in several positions. This mobility of adverb position allows the speaker or writer to emphasize different words within the sentence:

They watered their lawn *frequently.*

Frequently, they watered their lawn.

They *frequently* watered their lawn.

For more details about adverbs, see section 12C.

9D Words that relate and connect

Conjunctions

A conjunction joins words, phrases, and clauses together. There are three types of conjunctions: coordinating conjunctions, correlative conjunctions, and subordinating conjunctions.

1. **Coordinating conjunctions** connect words and groups of words in such a way that they are given equal emphasis and importance to the reader or listener. The coordinating conjunctions are **and, but, for, or,** and **yet.**

   Jessica *and* Peter both chose the homeless as a topic.

   Taft *and* Canoga Park High Schools will receive more students next semester.

   I plan to travel to Norway *or* to Switzerland.

2. **Subordinating conjunctions** introduce subordinate clauses, and, in doing so, subordinate the *ideas* of the clauses. Some of the many subordinating conjunctions are **if, unless, before, after, because, when, until, as, since.**

   We seldom buy gasoline *where* they refuse to post the octane.

Before you choose a college, visit each campus on your list.

Because my whole family will be away this holiday, I will visit my sister.

3. **Correlative conjunctions** each are comprised of two or more words that act together. They work very much like coordinating conjunctions, because they link equal elements in a sentence. The correlative conjunctions are **either. . .or, both. . .and, neither. . . nor, whether. . .or, not only. . .but (also).**

   I would like to travel *either* to France *or* to North Carolina this summer.

   The team could not decide *whether* to use the running game *or* to attempt some long passes.

For more details about connectives, see section 14.

Prepositions

A preposition is a word that relates a noun or pronoun to another word, usually in regard to **position, direction, space, cause,** or **time**: *under* the sea, *on* a ledge, *within* the pages, *between* you and me, *by* the composer, *after* the game, *during* the lecture, *among* the children, *of* the nation.

For more details about prepositions, see section 15.

9E Words that express emotion: Interjections

Interjections are words that express surprise or emotion. They can stand by themselves, or they may be followed by a closely related sentence.

Good grief!

Oh, no! I forgot the plane tickets.

For more details about exclamations, see section 16.

10 NOUN

A noun is a part of speech that identifies people, places, objects, actions, and ideas.

PEOPLE:

Michael Douglas, Bill Clinton, girl, baker, scoutmaster

PLACES:

Hawaii, Chicago, the lake, downtown, school

OBJECTS:

car, toaster, lawn mower, fighter-bomber, ring

ACTIONS:

persuasion, sale, completion, winning, invention

IDEAS:

liberty, justice, honesty, symmetry, democracy

CONCEPTS:

women's rights, apartheid, affirmative action, *glasnost*

Nouns function as subjects, objects, complements, appositives, and sometimes modifiers. The articles *a, an,* and *the* are noun determiners that signal that a noun is to follow. The suffixes *-ence, -ance, -ation, -ism, -ity, -ness,* and *-ship* are frequently used to create nouns from other parts of speech. The English language has a vast accumulation of nouns, which can be arranged into several classifications.

10A Batch nouns and countable nouns

Batch nouns are those that identify things that cannot be divided into separate units, like *milk, sugar, salt, dirt, meat,* and *oxygen.* Countable nouns are easily separated into individual units, like *presents, children, eggs, oranges,* and *books.*

10B Abstract and concrete nouns

Abstract nouns identify qualities, concepts, and emotions that cannot be perceived through the senses, like *freedom, resolution, willingness, fear, annoyance,* and *thoughtfulness.* On the other hand, concrete nouns can be touched, seen, smelled, heard, tasted: *ice cream, television, ship,* and *turnpike.*

10C Proper and common nouns

Because proper nouns refer to particular names and titles, they are always capitalized. Nouns such as *Beverly Hills, Hillary Clinton, Thanksgiving Day,* and *Yellowstone Park* are capitalized; they seldom take an article, although it is proper to say *the Bill of Rights* or *the Los Angeles River.*

10D Collective nouns

Nouns which identify groups of persons, animals, or things are usually considered singular, unless reference is clearly to the parts of the noun.

SINGULAR:

class, crowd, congregation, mob, audience, battalion

PLURAL:

The majority were women.

10E Nominals

Nominals are words and groups of words that function as nouns, although they are not nouns. Foremost among these are pronouns, but there are others as well:

ADJECTIVE:

The story was about the *young* and the *restless.*

GERUND:

Losing weight is difficult for those over thirty.

INFINITIVE:

He wanted *to surprise the entire office staff.*

PREPOSITIONS:

The *ups* and *downs* of life haunted the bodybuilder.

PRONOUNS:

She wanted a chance to be an administrator.

11 VERB

A verb is a word that shows action or state of being. Grammatically, the verb is the most important word in the sentence; from it are derived sentence form and structure. Look at the three sentences which follow:

1. Oleg **rebelled.** (intransitive verb)
2. Oleg **painted** his garage. (transitive verb)
3. Oleg **was** a Russian soldier. (linking verb)

All verbs are one of three types: transitive, intransitive, and linking.

11A Intransitive verbs do not take objects

The emphasis in sentences with intransitive verbs is on the action that the subject performs. Here are examples of S-V sentences, or PATTERN I sentences:

Maria giggled.

Little Jimmy rebelled.

Elizabeth fainted.

Murray shaves.

The teacher objected.

Of course, we do not often write or say such short sentences. Usually we add adverbial modifiers (which explain *how, where, when,* or *why* the action is performed):

Maria **giggled**, *on and off, for the rest of the hour.*

Little Jimmy **rebelled** *when he was made to eat spinach.*

Elizabeth **fainted** *at the news of UCLA's defeat.*

Murray **shaves** *whenever he has a job interview.*

The teacher **objected** *to the students' performing a wave in class.*

Notice that such adverbial modifiers still do not change the structure of the sentence. The subject is performing an action, and there is no receiver of the action, or direct object. The adverbial phrases and clauses simply modify or describe the action.

11B Transitive verbs, as their very name signifies, *transfer* action from the subject to another noun in the sentence called the direct object

Where does the direct object come from? It is put there by the writer of the sentence, because once that writer uses a transitive verb, the sentence must have a receiver of the action, or direct object. Here are some examples of S-V-DO sentences (or PATTERN II sentences):

Maria **bought** some writing paper.

Hai **stitched** her dress.

Elmer **wanted** a Mustang.

Bill **ate** a hamburger.

Cynthia **kicked** each tire.

11C Linking verbs express little action; mainly they express state of being, and link the subject to a complement (called a predicate noun or predicate adjective) following the verb

By far, the most used linking verb is the verb *to be*, in all of its forms. Some other linking verbs are *looks, appears, seems, grows, becomes,* and *feels*. Here are some S-V-PN\PA sentences, called PATTERN III sentences:

The cats **became** hungry.
Bruno **looks** exhausted.
Paula **feels** sick.
John **is** a doctor.
Bill **was** an expert marksman.

In these ways, verbs control every aspect of the sentence. See Sentence Structure, section 20, for more discussion of sentence formation.

11D Principal parts of verbs

All verbs have four principal parts: the *present* (NOW), the *past* (YESTERDAY), the *present participle* (the -ING form of the verb), and the *past participle* (the form of the verb with HAVE). To find the principal parts of a verb, just remember the clues NOW, YESTERDAY, -ING, and HAVE.

PRESENT:

(you) *work* (NOW)

PAST:

(you) *worked* (YESTERDAY)

PRESENT PARTICIPLE:

(you are) *workING*

PAST PARTICIPLE:

(you HAVE) *worked*

PRESENT:

(he) *buys* (NOW)

PAST:

(he) *bought* (YESTERDAY)

PRESENT PARTICIPLE:

(he is) *buyING*

PAST PARTICIPLE:

(he HAS) *bought*

Participles are used both:

1. as part of the main verb of the sentence

and

2. as other parts of speech, like nouns and adjectives.

When the main verb is separated from its helping verbs (like *has, have, be, does*) by intervening parts of a sentence, sometimes, through omission, an error in verb formation results. The verb formation *did not swum*, for example, is obviously wrong when seen out of context, but notice how difficult it is to spot in a sentence.

INCORRECT:

Florence Chadwick *had swum* the English Channel twice before in treacherously cold weather, but last winter she *did not*.

CORRECT:

Florence Chadwick *had swum* the English Channel twice before in treacherously cold weather, but last winter she *did not swim*.

INCORRECT:

The rebel groups never *have* and never *will surrender* to any government forces.

CORRECT:

The rebel groups never *have surrendered* and never *will surrender* to any government forces.

3. Another error involving principal parts of verbs results from a confusion of the simple past and the past participle. As in the preceding examples, such errors are more likely to occur in sentences where subject and verb are separated by modifiers. Note the following examples:

Examples	Present	Past	Past Participle
We *saw* (not *seen*) the dog just last week.	see	saw	seen
The Dodgers finally *did* (not *done*) it.	do	did	done
My family had *gone* (not *went*) there for several summers.	go	went	gone
The music *began* (not *begun*) as the ship slid into the sea.	begin	began	begun
Jose Canseco had *broken* (not *broke*) his favorite bat.	break	broke	broken
The guests had *eaten* (not *ate*) before the wedding party arrived.	eat	ate	eaten
The Liberty Bell had *rung* (not *rang*) every Fourth of July for a century.	ring	rang	rung

4. Verbs like *sit, set, rise, raise, lie,* and *lay* cause trouble because of similarity of form.

Examples	Present	Past	Past Participle
My cats usually *lie* (not *lay*) in the sun.	lie (to recline)	lay	lain
The president *lay* (not *laid*) down for his afternoon rest.			

Examples	Present	Past	Past Participle
The wounded soldier had *lain* (not *laid*) on the battlefield for three days.			
If you *lay* (not *lie*) your jacket on the counter, it may become soiled.	lay (to place)	laid	laid
Phillip *laid* (not *lay*) the new sod on the prepared soil.			
The contractors have recently *laid* (not *lain*) the fresh cement for our new driveway.			
At the sound of "Hail to the Chief" everyone usually *rises* (not *raises*).	rise (to get up or move up)	rose	risen
The flag *rose* (not *raised*) to the strains of "The Marine Hymn."			
We feel that the faculty and staff have *risen* (not *raised*) to the challenge.			
The college trustees intend to *raise* (not *rise*) student fees.	raise (to cause to rise)	raised	raised
The students *raised* (not *rose*) the dress-code issue again.			
The neighbors had *raised* (not *risen*) the third side of the barn by noon.			

5. Some errors arise from the confusion of the present tense with another principal part. These errors very often arise from mispronunciation of the words.

EXAMPLES:

The students protested that the test was *supposed* (not *suppose*) to be on Chapter Three.

They *used* (not *use*) to have dinner together every Friday.

Shirley *came* (not *come*) to see how you are.

6. The following list of principal parts features verbs that sometimes cause trouble in speaking and writing.

Present	Past	Past Participle
become	became	become
begin	began	begun
bid (offer)	bid	bid
bid (command)	bade	bidden
bite	bit	bit, bitten
blow	blew	blown

Present	Past	Past Participle
break	broke	broken
bring	brought	brought
burst	burst	burst
catch	caught	caught
choose	chose	chosen
come	came	come
dive	dived, dove	dived
do	did	done
drag	dragged	dragged
draw	drew	drawn
drink	drank	drunk
drive	drove	driven
eat	ate	eaten
fall	fell	fallen
fly	flew	flown
forget	forgot	forgot, forgotten
freeze	froze	frozen
get	got	got, gotten
give	gave	given
go	went	gone
grow	grew	grown
hang (suspend)	hung	hung
hang (execute)	hanged	hanged
know	knew	known
lay	laid	laid
lead	led	led
lend	lent	lent
lie (recline)	lay	lain
lie (speak falsely)	lied	lied
lose	lost	lost
pay	paid	paid
prove	proved	proved, proven
raise	raised	raised
ride	rode	ridden
ring	rang, rung	rung
rise	rose	risen
run	ran	run
see	saw	seen
shake	shook	shaken
shrink	shrank	shrunk
sing	sang, sung	sung
sink	sank, sunk	sunk
speak	spoke	spoken
spring	sprang	sprung
steal	stole	stolen
swim	swam	swum

Present	Past	Past Participle
swing	swung	swung
take	took	taken
tear	tore	torn
throw	threw	thrown
wear	wore	worn
weave	wove	woven
wring	wrung	wrung
write	wrote	written

11E Tense and mood

A verb shows the time (or tense) of the action by changing its form. A **conjugation** is an intact list of all the forms of a verb by *mood, number, person, tense,* and *voice.* A synopsis is a summary of these forms in only one person, as displayed below for the verb *tell.*

Each verb form expresses a different shade of meaning. **Simple** forms show the everyday norm; **progressive** forms indicate action in progress at any particular time; **emphatic** forms add a degree of emphasis, and are mainly used in questions. The **imperative mood** issues commands ("Tell us the answers"). The **subjunctive mood** indicates wishing ("I wish it were being told now"), a condition contrary to fact ("If the story were told now, there would be a riot"), and sometimes urgency ("They insist that they be told the facts now").

INDICATIVE MOOD
Simple Form

Tense	Active Voice	Passive Voice
Present	they tell	they are told
Past	they told	they were told
Future	they will tell	they will be told
Present perfect	they have told	they have been told
Past perfect	they had told	they had been told
Future perfect	they will have told	they will have been told

Progressive Form

Tense	Active Voice	Passive Voice
Present	they are telling	they are being told
Past	they were telling	they were being told
Future	they will be telling	they will be told
Present perfect	they have been telling	they have been told
Past perfect	they had been telling	they had been told
Future perfect	they will have been telling	they will have been told

Emphatic Form

Tense	Active Voice Only
Present	they do tell
Past	they did tell

IMPERATIVE MOOD
Used only in the second person, present tense

	Active Voice	Passive Voice
	(you) tell	(you) be told

SUBJUNCTIVE MOOD
Simple Form

Tense	Active Voice	Passive Voice
Present	(if) they tell	(if) they be told
Past	(if) they told	(if) they were told
Future	(if) they will tell	(if) they will be told
Present perfect	(if) they have told	(if) they have been told
Past perfect	(if) they had told	(if) they had been told
Future perfect	(if) they will have told	(if) they will have been told

11F Tense, shift in tense

A verb in a subordinate clause should relate logically in tense to the verb in the principal clause. Avoid any unnecessary shift.

INCORRECT:

As the wedding *began* [past], the bride's mother *starts* [present] to cry.

CORRECT:

As the wedding *began* [past], the bride's mother *started* [past] to cry.

INCORRECT:

He *had intended* [past perfect] to finish his third novel by the end of the year, but he *has been very sick* [present perfect] until Thanksgiving.

CORRECT:

He *had intended* [past perfect] to finish his third novel by the end of the year, but he *had been very sick* [past perfect] until Thanksgiving.

INCORRECT:

By the time the fire *had been extinguished* [past perfect], the priceless paintings *had been destroyed* [past perfect].

CORRECT:

By the time the fire *was extinguished* [past], the priceless paintings *had been destroyed* [past perfect]. (The past perfect expresses action that took place before the simple past.)

Because *tense* indicates the time of the action and *voice* indicates whether the subject is the agent of the action (*active:* Tom *saw*) or the recipient of the action (*passive:* Tom *was seen*), both of these verb forms are central to the consistency of a sentence or passage.

11G Voice

A verb in a subordinate clause should relate logically in voice to the verb in the main clause. It is generally better to avoid voice shifts within a sentence.

INCORRECT:

Sighs of appreciation *could be heard* [passive] as the waiters *brought* [active] huge trays of roast beef and Yorkshire pudding.

REVISED:

The guests *sighed* [active] with appreciation as the waiters *brought* [active] huge trays of roast beef and Yorkshire pudding.

INCORRECT:

If the fishing boat *had been reached* [passive] in time, the Coast Guard *might have saved* [active] it with floats. (Note that the subject shifts as well as the voice.)

REVISED:

If it *had reached* [active] the fishing boat in time, the Coast Guard *might have saved* [active] it with floats.

11H Present infinitive

Always use the present infinitive (*to run, to see*) after a perfect tense (a tense that uses some form of the helping verb *have* or *had*).

EXAMPLES:

He *has decided to order* the Jaguar Model S-1. (Present Perfect + Present Infinitive).

They *had hoped to hold* a spring picnic. (Past Perfect + Present Infinitive)

11I Subjunctive mood

Verbs may be expressed in one of three moods: the *indicative*, used to declare a fact or ask a question; the *imperative*, used to express a command; and the *subjunctive*, generally used to indicate doubt or to express a wish or request or a condition contrary to fact. The first two moods are fairly clear-cut.

INDICATIVE:

This cake is tasty. Who baked it?

IMPERATIVE:

Please leave now. Go home.

NOTE:

The imperative mood has only one subject (you) and one tense (the present).

SUBJUNCTIVE:

The subjunctive mood presents more of a problem. It suggests *possibilities, maybes, could have beens,* or *wishes that it had been,* and its uses are sometimes more difficult to understand. The subjunctive mood appears more frequently in formal English than in standard written English.

Notice the following uses, including some traditional ones.

EXAMPLES:

I insist that the new road *be started* this spring.

The company requires that the check *be certified*.

Had she *been* certain of her facts, she would have challenged the teacher.

If need *be,* we can use our pension money.

Should the swarm *reappear,* I will call a beekeeper.

If he *were* honest, he would return all the money.

I move that the budget *be accepted*.

Far *be* it from me to suggest that he is lying.

Would that I *were* sixteen again!

I wish I *were* on a plane to Tahiti.

NOTE:

Today, the subjunctive is most often used to express doubt, wishes, or conditions contrary to fact. However, the indicative can also be used for some of these same feelings.

SUBJUNCTIVE MOOD:

If it *be* true, I will be delighted.

INDICATIVE MOOD:

If it *is* true, I will be delighted.

11J Special use of the present tense

Use the present tense to express universally true statements or timeless facts.

EXAMPLES:

Ice *forms* at 32°F.

The rainy season seldom *arrives* in California.

She told the campers that mosquitoes *are* part of nature.

11K Historical present

In writing about a poem or describing events in fiction or plays, use the present tense. This convention is called the *historical present*.

EXAMPLE:

In *A Tale of Two Cities,* Dr. Manette *is restored to* his daughter after twenty years in jail.

11L Verb forms and verbals

A high percentage of verb-related errors occurs because the reader confuses *verb forms*—that is, the different forms that an action word can assume—with entirely different structures known as *verbals*—words formed from verbs but not used as verbs in a sentence. Known as *participles, gerunds,* and *infinitives,* verbals form important phrases within the sentence.

1. Infinitives

An infinitive is ordinarily preceded by *to* and is used as a noun, an adjective, or an adverb.

NOUN:

> *To err* is human. (Subject)

ADJECTIVE:

> The survivors had little *to celebrate*. (*To celebrate* modifies the noun *little*.)

ADVERB:

> *To please* his children, Jerry bought a new pool. (*To please* modifies the verb *bought*.)

Sometimes, infinitives omit the word *to*.

EXAMPLES:

> Who dares [to] *challenge* a champion?
>
> Please [to] *go*.
>
> Make him [to] *turn* on the radio.
>
> We saw him [to] *leave*.

2. Gerunds

Because both gerunds and participles have an *-ing* ending, they can be harder to distinguish between. However, a sentence that equates the two presents an error in parallel structure. If you understand the function of each in the sentence, you will be sure to spot this error.

A gerund always ends in *-ing* and functions as a noun.

SUBJECT:

> *Writing* is very rewarding.

SUBJECTIVE COMPLEMENT:

> My favorite occupation is *binding* books.

DIRECT OBJECT:

> He now regrets *resigning*.

OBJECT OF PREPOSITION:

> After *sealing* the letter, he went for a walk.

3. Participles

A participle acts as an adjective in the sentence.

EXAMPLES:

> *Growling threateningly*, the gorilla intimidated the crowd. (Growling modifies gorilla.)
> The floor *invaded by termites* was made of oak. (Invaded modifies floor.)

There are two forms of participles, present and past. Present participles end in *-ing*; past participles assume many different forms (e.g., *bought, granted, shown, heard, hung, hidden, shot, torn*).

Also see *Phrases* 20F and *Dangling Constructions* 12E.

11M Passive voice

Other verb forms that may give trouble are the progressive and the passive. Progressive verb forms are regular

action words that emphasize continuing action: "I *am running*" rather than "I *run*." Passive verbs transform the sentence in such a way that the subject is receiving action instead of performing it: "I *was given*" instead of "I *gave*."

Note the similarities of form in the following groups.

VERBS:

> *Simple*—I *hit* the clay target fifty times.
>
> *Progressive*—I *am hitting* the ball better than ever.
>
> *Passive*—I *was hit* by a snowball.

VERBALS:

> *Infinitive*—*To hit* a child is considered criminal.
>
> *Gerund*—*Hitting* golf balls at a driving range is essential preparation for a match.
>
> *Participle*—The man *hitting the ball* is also the coach.

12 MODIFIERS

12A Adjectives and adverbs

The purpose of adjectives and adverbs is to describe, limit, color—in other words, to *modify* other words. Adjectives modify nouns or pronouns, and generally precede the words they modify. Adverbs describe verbs, adjectives or other adverbs. Some words can be used as either adjectives (He has an *early appointment*) or adverbs (He *arrived early*).

ADJECTIVES:

> *fuzzy* peach
>
> *impressive* view
>
> *sour* milk

ADVERBS:

> He grumbled *loudly*.
>
> She smiled *broadly*.
>
> It poured *unmercifully*.

Although most adverbs end in *-ly*, some do not (*fast, hard, long, straight*). A few adjectives also have an *-ly* ending (*lovely* day, *lively* discussion).

12B Adjectives

Problems that students face with adjectives frequently relate to the use of degrees of comparison. There are three degrees: the *positive*—the original form of the word (*straight*); the *comparative*—used to compare two persons or things (*straighter*); and the superlative—used to compare more than two persons or things (*straightest*). If not understood, the spelling and form changes involved can sometimes confuse the unwary student.

1. Most adjectives form the comparative and superlative degrees by adding *-er* and *-est*:

POSITIVE:

> nice

COMPARATIVE:

nicer

SUPERLATIVE:

nicest

2. Other adjectives form the comparative and superlative by using *more* and *most:*

POSITIVE:

challenging

COMPARATIVE:

more challenging

SUPERLATIVE:

most challenging

3. Some adjectives change completely as they form the comparative and superlative degrees.

POSITIVE:

little   good

COMPARATIVE:

less   better

SUPERLATIVE:

least   best

Be alert for double comparisons, which incorrectly use *more* or *most* with adjectives that already express a degree: *more softer* or *most strongest.*

INCORRECT:

He was the most gentlest doctor I have ever seen.

CORRECT:

He was the gentlest doctor I have ever seen.

Also, watch for the illogical use of the comparative or the superlative with adjectives that cannot be compared, such as *square, round, perfect, unique.* It is meaningless to write *rounder* or *most perfect.*

When comparing only two nouns, use the comparative degree: Mars is the *larger* of the two planets. When comparing more than two, use the superlative: Canseco is the *most dangerous* hitter on their team.

12C Adverbs

Adverbs (either as words, phrases, or clauses) describe the words they modify by indicating *when, how, where, why, in what order,* or *how often.*

WHEN:

He studied *until* 10:00 every night.

HOW:

She testified *quietly* and with dignity.

WHERE:

Bring the paper *here.*

WHY:

They rejected the offer *because* it was too little.

IN WHAT ORDER:

One *after* another, the townspeople told the judge their story.

NOTE:

Anywheres, nowheres, and *somewheres* are incorrect adverb forms. Use *anywhere, nowhere, somewhere.*

The adjectives *good* and *bad* should not be used as adverbs.

NOT

She doesn't sing so *good.*

He wants that job *bad.*

BUT

She doesn't sing so *well.*

He wants that job *badly.*

Standard English requires the use of a formal adverb form rather than a colloquial version.

NOT

This was a *real* good clambake.

He *sure* doesn't look happy.

BUT

This was a *really* good clambake.

He *surely* doesn't look happy.

12D Misplaced modifiers

Probably the most persistent and frustrating errors in the English language involve either *incorrect modification* or else *inexact modification* that is difficult to pin down.

In most cases, if you can keep your eye on the *word or phrase being modified,* it is easier to avoid the following pitfalls.

To avoid confusion or ambiguity, place the modifying words, phrases, or clauses near the words they modify.

1. Misplaced Adverb Modifiers

Adverbs like *scarcely, nearly, merely, just, even,* and *almost* must be placed near the words they modify.

CONFUSED:

Last week during the cold spell, I *nearly* lost all of my flowers.

CLEAR:

Last week during the cold spell, I lost *nearly* all of my flowers. (The adverb *nearly* modifies the pronoun *all.*)

CONFUSED:

Acme *just* cleaned my rugs last month.

CLEAR:

Acme cleaned my rugs *just* last month. (The adverb *just* modifies the adverbial phrase *last month.*)

2. Misplaced Phrase Modifiers

CONFUSED:

To plant tomatoes, it was a good growing year.

CLEAR:

It was a good growing year *to plant tomatoes.*

CONFUSED:

Like a sleek projectile, the passengers saw the new train approach the station.

CLEAR:

The passengers saw the new train approach the station *like a sleek projectile.*

3. Misplaced Clause Modifiers

CONFUSED:

He packed all of his books and documents into his van, *which he was donating to the library.*

CLEAR:

He packed all of his books and documents, *which he was donating to the library,* into his van.

CONFUSED:

The new series of seminars will focus on how to prevent inflation, *which will benefit us all.*

CLEAR:

The new series of seminars, *which will benefit us all,* will focus on how to prevent inflation.

12E Dangling constructions

A dangling modifier literally hangs in the air; there is no logical word in the sentence for it to modify. Frequently it is placed close to the wrong noun or verb, causing the sentence to sound ridiculous: *Driving through the park, several chipmunks could be seen.*

1. Dangling Participles

A participle is a form of the verb that is used as an adjective. Unless there is a logical word for it to modify, the participial phrase will dangle, modifying either the wrong noun or none at all.

INCORRECT:

Having run out of gas, John was late for dinner.

REVISED:

Because the car ran out of gas, John was late for dinner.

INCORRECT:

Standing outside for a quick smoke, deer were spotted.

REVISED:

Standing outside for a quick smoke, we spotted several deer.

2. Dangling Gerunds

A gerund is the *-ing* form of a verb serving as a noun (*Smoking is bad for our health*). When a gerund is used as the object of a preposition ("by *hiding,*" "after *escaping,*" "upon *realizing*"), the phrase can dangle if the actor that it modifies is missing.

INCORRECT:

After putting a bloodworm on my hook, the flounders began to bite.

REVISED:

After putting a bloodworm on my hook, I found that the flounders began to bite.

INCORRECT:

In designing our house addition, a bathroom was forgotten.

REVISED:

In designing our house addition, we forgot to add a bathroom.

3. Dangling Infinitives

Unlike the participle and the gerund, the infinitive performs more than one job in a sentence. While the participle acts like an adjective, and the gerund like a noun, the infinitive phrase can take the part of a noun, adjective, or adverb. Note the following examples of dangling infinitive phrases.

INCORRECT:

To skate like a champion, practice is essential.

REVISED:

To skate like a champion, one must practice.

INCORRECT:

To make a good impression, a shirt and tie should be worn to the interview.

REVISED:

To make a good impression, Jeff should wear a shirt and tie to the interview.

12F Illogical comparisons

Occasionally, a writer will mistakenly compare items that are not comparable.

INCORRECT:

Her *salary* was lower than a *clerk.* (The *salary* is incorrectly compared with a *clerk.*)

CORRECT:

Her *salary* was lower than a *clerk's.*

INCORRECT:

The cultural *events* in Orlando are as diversified as *any other large city.* (*Events* are being compared with a *large city.*)

CORRECT:

The cultural *events* in Orlando are as diversified as *those in any other large city.*

Another form of illogical comparison results when a writer fails to exclude from the rest of the group the item being compared.

INCORRECT:

She is taller than *any girl* in her class.

CORRECT:

She is taller than *any other girl* in her class.

13 PRONOUNS

Pronouns are most often employed as substitutes for nouns, but some can also be used as adjectives or conjunctions. To master pronouns and be able to spot errors in their use, you need to understand pronoun *case* (nominative, possessive, objective), pronoun *number* (singular or plural), and pronoun *class* (personal, demonstrative, interrogative, relative, indefinite).

13A Personal pronouns

A personal pronoun indicates by its form the person or thing it takes the place of: the person speaking (first person), the person spoken to (second person), or the person or thing spoken about (third person).

	Singular	Plural
First-Person Pronouns		
Nominative case	I	we
Possessive case	my, mine	our, ours
Objective case	me	us
Second-Person Pronouns		
Nominative case	you	you
Possessive case	your, yours	your, yours
Objective case	you	you
Third-Person Pronouns		
Nominative case	he, she, it	they
Possessive case	his, her, hers, its	their, theirs
Objective case	him, her, it	them

Some common errors in pronoun case occur frequently in everyday speech. Study the following applications to see if you have been using the correct forms.

1. Use the nominative case of a pronoun in a compound subject.

EXAMPLE:

Betty and I watched the Olympics on television.

2. Use the nominative case of a pronoun following any form of the verb *to be*.

This use may just not sound all right to you, but it is standard American usage. The use of a pronoun in the objective case here, as in *Betty and me...*, would flatly be incorrect.

EXAMPLES:

It is *she*.　The winner was *I*.

3. Use the objective case when the pronoun is the object of a preposition.

EXAMPLES:

This is just between you and *me*.

Doug looks like *me*. (*Like*, as well as *but*, can be used as a preposition.)

Nadine made coffee for Allan, Ken, and *me*.

When there are intervening words, eliminate them to find the correct pronoun to use. "Nadine made coffee for *I*" sounds ridiculous, yet some people might say, "Nadine made coffee for Allan, Ken, and *I*." Similarly, in the sentence (*We*) (*Us*) *homeowners want better roads,*" eliminate the word homeowners to find the correct word: "*We want better roads*."

4. Use the objective case when the pronoun is the object of a verb.

EXAMPLE:

The noise frightened Karen and *me*.

5. Use the nominative case for pronouns that are subjects of elliptical clauses (clauses that are incomplete or unexpressed).

At times, we leave words out because they are not necessary for the comprehension of the sentence. Such missing words are called *ellipses*. In the sentence, "You are a better player than he," the writer or speaker is really saying, "You are a better player than he *is*." Notice that, unless we keep in mind the complete thought, it is very easy to finish the sentence with the incorrect "...than *him*." "You are a better player than *him*" is incorrect because the objective pronoun *him* cannot be used as a subject ("You are a better player than *him* is"). That job is reserved for the nominative pronoun, *he*.

EXAMPLES:

My children are as excited as *I* [am].

She raked more than *he* [raked].

As and *than* are subordinating conjunctions that introduce elliptical clauses. Complete the clause to determine the pronoun case.

6. Use a possessive pronoun before a gerund. Just as you would say *My* car, you would also say *My* smoking bothers her.

EXAMPLE:

We have always regretted *her* leaving for California.

Possessive Pronoun-Gerund Combination Drill

If you have the habit of using objective-case pronouns with gerunds and gerund phrases, a very common error, try to remember this: *Gerunds are always nouns; therefore any pronoun placed before them must always be a possessive pronoun.* Here is an easy way to develop an ear for the use of the correct pronoun case. The following sentences are all correct. Just read the list several times, preferably aloud.

1. She resented *my* going out and having business lunches.

2. The girls were irritated at *our* referring to the old fraternity all evening.

3. *Your* car-pooling can help rid the city of gridlock.

4. Edna began to feel embarrassed at *his* jumping into every conversation and immediately monopolizing it.

5. *Our* letting Brock eat table scraps from the table produced a spoiled animal.

6. *Your* sponsoring our son will not be forgotten.

7. *My* getting married should have no impact on you.

8. He felt strongly that he did not have to explain *his* enlisting in the Navy to anyone.

9. *Their* treating of oil as the only economical source of energy has brought us to a critical state of dependence.

10. *Her* brushing her hair every night has certainly made a difference in her appearance.

11. *Her* knowing that he did not have much money, yet ordering prime rib and lobster tails, was an example of raw greed.

12. Mary thinks *his* chewing gum is the reason he did not get the part.

13. *Her* losing her wallet started off a very bad day.

14. The whole city was shocked by *his* refusing to take the oath.

15. *My* taking lunch to work every day has saved hundreds of dollars so far.

13B Demonstrative pronouns

Demonstrative pronouns (*this, that, these, those*) take the place of things being pointed out.

EXAMPLES:

These are Mary's.

I don't like *this.*

They are called demonstrative adjectives when used before nouns: *These seats* are comfortable.

INCORRECT:

Them are the new watches I ordered.

CORRECT:

Those are the new watches I ordered. (Demonstrative pronoun)

Do not substitute a personal pronoun for a demonstrative pronoun or a demonstrative adjective.

INCORRECT:

Look at *them* diamonds!

CORRECT:

Look at *those* diamonds! (Demonstrative adjective)

13C Interrogative pronouns

Interrogative pronouns (*who, whom, whose, which,* and *what*) are used in questions. *Who, which,* and *what* are

used as subjects and are in the nominative case. *Whose* is in the possessive case. *Whom* is in the objective case, and, like all objects, it is the receiver of action in the sentence.

The most common error involving interrogative pronouns is the tendency to use *who* instead of *whom.*

1. When the pronoun is receiving the action, the objective form *whom* must be used.

INCORRECT:

Who did you contact?

CORRECT:

Whom did you contact? (You did contact whom?)

2. When the pronoun is performing the action, the nominative *who* must be used.

INCORRECT:

Whom did you say is running the dance?

CORRECT:

Who did you say is running the dance?

(*Who* is the subject of *is running.*)

13D Relative pronouns

Relative pronouns (*who, whom, whose, which, what,* and *that*) refer to people and things. When a relative pronoun is the subject of a subordinate clause, the clause becomes an adjective modifying a noun in the sentence.

EXAMPLE:

The rumor that plagued him all his life was a lie. (*That plagued him all his life* modifies *rumor.*)

Which and *that* can also act as conjunctions to introduce subordinate clauses.

EXAMPLE:

Bob knew *that* Boston would win.

Remember that the case of a relative pronoun is established by its function inside its clause:

Aimee is the girl *who* needs your advice. (*Who* is the subject of the verb *needs* within the clause.)

Coach Shanks is the person *whom* we must thank. (*Whom* is the object of *must thank* within the clause.)

You can give the relief supplies to *whomever* you choose. (The noun clause is the object of the preposition *to; whomever* is the object of the verb *choose* within the clause.)

Do not let intervening parenthetical expressions like "*I imagine*" or "*for sure*" mislead you.

There are some customers *whom*, I would guess, you can never please.

For sure, *whoever comes first* is very welcome.

13E Indefinite pronouns

Indefinite pronouns (*all, another, any, both, each, either, everyone, many, neither, one, several, some,* and similar words) represent an indefinite number of persons or things. Many of these words also function as adjectives ("*several* men").

Indefinite pronouns present few problems. One thing to remember:

1. Use a singular pronoun with an indefinite antecedent like *one, everyone,* and *anybody.*

INCORRECT:

Everyone needs to prepare *themselves* for retirement.

CORRECT:

Everyone needs to prepare *himself* (or *herself*) for retirement.

And a final caution:

2. The antecedent of a pronoun should be clear, specific, and close to the pronoun. Reword the sentence if necessary.

CONFUSING:

The coach told Eric that *he* could practice after school.

CLEAR:

The coach said that Eric could practice after school.

14 CONNECTIVES

14A Connectives that join elements of equal rank are called coordinating conjunctions (*and, but, or, nor, for, yet*)

Connectives that introduce a less important element are called *subordinating conjunctions* (after, although, since, when).

Coordinating conjunctions link words, phrases, and clauses that are of equal importance.

EXAMPLES:

The pilot *and* the crew boarded the plane.
The road ran through the valley *and* along the river.

Compound sentences are formed when coordinating conjunctions link two independent clauses.

EXAMPLE:

You can sign the loan papers on Friday, *or* you can sign them on Monday.

14B *Subordinating conjunctions* are used in sentences to connect clauses that are not equal in rank—that is, in sentences in which one idea is made subordinate to another

There are many subordinating conjunctions. Some of the important ones are *after, as, because, before, if, in order*

that, once, since, unless, until, whenever, and *wherever.*

EXAMPLES:

We covered up the newly planted citrus trees *when* the temperature began to drop.

Until I saw her in person, I thought Cher was a tall woman.

14C Another form of connective is the *conjunctive adverb.* It is actually an adverb that functions as a coordinating conjunction

The principal conjunctive adverbs are *accordingly, also, besides, certainly, consequently, finally, furthermore, however, incidentally, instead, likewise, nevertheless, otherwise, similarly,* and *undoubtedly.* When they join clauses, conjunctive adverbs are usually preceded by a semicolon and followed by a comma.

EXAMPLE:

I understand you wish to see a Broadway musical; *undoubtedly,* you'll have to get tickets far in advance for one of the hit shows.

Coordination can be overdone. If every significant idea in every sentence is given equal weight, there is no main idea.

15 PREPOSITIONS

A preposition is a word that relates a noun or pronoun to another word, usually in regard to position, direction, space, cause, or time: *under* the sea, *on* a ledge, *within* the pages, *between* you and me, *by* the composer, *after* the game, *during* the lecture, *among* the children, *of* the nation. A preposition always has an object, which is usually a noun or pronoun; the combination of preposition and object is called a *prepositional phrase.*

President Kennedy knew *with certainty* that there were missiles *in Cuba.*

Other common prepositions:

at	above	across	around	about
besides	before	behind	below	by
for	from	in	inside	of
on	onto	over	off	round
through	till	to	toward	up

16 INTERJECTIONS

Exclamations that express emotions or surprise are called interjections. They are usually emotives like *Ouch!, Wow!, Stop it!, Fire!,* or *Help!* Grammatically, interjections are considered self-contained sentences.

17 SUBJECT-VERB AGREEMENT

Nouns, verbs, and pronouns often have special forms or endings that indicate *number*—that is, whether the word is singular or plural. A verb must agree in number with the noun or pronoun that is its subject.

17A A verb agrees in number with its subject

A singular subject requires a singular verb; a plural subject, a plural verb.

Singular	Plural
The *house has* three bathrooms.	Many *houses have* more than one bathroom.
UCLA is my choice.	*UCLA, Berkeley, and Stanford are* my favorites.
My cat, a Persian named Gus, *is* awake all night.	*Cats,* according to this article, *are* almost always nocturnal.
Mandy, together with the other girls, *wants* a pizza for lunch.	*Mandy and the other girls want* a pizza for lunch.

17B Do not let intervening words obscure the relationship between subject and verb

Find the subject and make the verb agree with it.

EXAMPLES:

A column of wounded prisoners, townspeople, and exhausted soldiers *was spotted* struggling over the horizon. (*Was spotted* agrees with its subject, *column,* not with the intervening plural nouns.)

She, her brother, and her friends from upstate *have* always *bought* tickets to the rock concert. (The verb agrees with the plural subject.)

17C Singular subjects followed by such words and phrases as *along with*, *as well as*, *in addition to*, *together with*, or *with* require singular verbs

EXAMPLE:

The *carrier,* together with three destroyers and two frigates, *was dispatched* to the Mediterranean Sea.

17D Indefinite pronouns like *anybody*, *each*, *either*, *everyone*, *neither*, and *one* are always singular, and take a singular verb, regardless of intervening words

Other indefinite pronouns, like *all, any, none,* or *some,* may be either singular or plural. *Both, few, many,* and *several* are always plural.

EXAMPLES:

Neither of my children *has* an interest in music.

All is not lost. BUT *All* of us *are going.*

Few of the golfers *were* professionals.

17E Compound subjects joined by *and* usually take a plural verb

(An exception is a compound subject that names one person, thing, or idea: *Ham and eggs* is a favorite breakfast.)

EXAMPLES:

The *Toyota* and the *Ford are* low on gas.

The *Pendletons,* the *Riveras,* and the *Kleins are coming to* dinner.

17F In sentences that begin with *there is* or *there are,* the subject follows the verb, and the verb must agree with it

EXAMPLES:

There *are* (verb) many *reasons* (subject) for the war in the Middle East.

17G Singular subjects joined by *or* or *nor* take a singular verb

If one subject is singular and the other plural, the verb should agree with the nearer subject

EXAMPLES:

Either the *vegetable* or the *pan is creating* this awful taste. (Singular subjects)

Either the *pan* or the *vegetables are creating* this awful taste. (The verb agrees with the nearer subject.)

17H Collective nouns (*bunch, committee, family, group, herd, jury, number, team*) may be either singular or plural, depending upon whether the group is regarded as a unit or as individuals

SINGULAR:

The *number* of homeless families *increases* every year.

The *committee has* the serious responsibility of selecting a new dean.

Notice that the same nouns are considered plural when the reference is to several individual members of the group.

PLURAL:

A *number* of homeless people *were* ill enough to require hospitalization.

The *committee have* not *agreed* on a date for the picnic.

NOTE:

A good rule to follow with *number, total,* and similar nouns is that, preceded by *the, number* is singular; preceded by *a,* it is plural. Another test: A *number of* should be treated as plural if it signifies several of many.

17I Words like *aeronautics, cybernetics, mathematics,* and *physics* or like *news* and *dollars,* are plural in form but usually singular in usage

EXAMPLES:

Mathematics is a subject essential to the sciences.

Eighty-five *dollars* for that coat *is* a bargain.

18 PRONOUN-ANTECEDENT AGREEMENT

18A Be sure that a singular pronoun is used with a singular antecedent (the word the pronoun refers to), that a plural pronoun is used with a plural antecedent, and that all pronouns and antecedents agree in number and gender

SINGULAR:

An author loves *his or her* fictional children.

PLURAL:

Girls love *their* Cabbage Patch dolls.

MASCULINE:

Steve loves *his* parents.

FEMININE:

Mabel loves *her* children.

1. Notice below that plural pronouns do not have gender, but that singular pronouns involve three choices:

	he	him	his	himself
Singular	she	her	her(s)	herself
	it	it	its	itself
Plural	they	them	their(s)	themselves

2. It is not acceptable to use the masculine pronouns to refer to both sexes as it once was.

A *teacher* must maintain *his* academic honesty.

Such sentences do not acknowledge women suitably and have come to suggest stereotypes. See *Sexist Language* in Section 32. The best way to correct such a sentence is to use a plural whenever possible, or to pair *his* or *her*.

Teachers must maintain *their* academic honesty.

OR

A *teacher* must maintain *his* or *her* academic honesty.

18B Singular words such as *man, woman, citizen, person, everybody, one, each, either, neither* take a singular pronoun

Each of these schools had *its* mascot changed. (NOT *their*)

One has to come to terms with *oneself*. (NOT *themselves*)

18C Compound antecedents joined by *and* are referred to by a plural pronoun

Peter and Ralph lost *their* way.

Both the bus and the truck missed *their* exit because of the fog.

18D Two or more singular antecedents joined by *or* or *nor* (or *either-or, neither-nor*) take a singular pronoun

Is it true that *neither Mitch nor Bill* passed *his* bar examination?

A *boy scout or even a cub scout* can take care of *himself* in the woods.

18E When antecedents differ in number and are joined by *or* or *nor* (or *either-or, neither-nor*), the pronoun agrees with the nearer antecedent

Neither the *soldier* nor the *prisoners* knew where *their* patrols were.

Many *anchovies* or even a great white *shark* has *its* struggles to survive in a hurricane at sea.

18F Collective nouns take singular or plural pronouns, depending on whether the noun is intended as a singular entity or plural entities

The *crowd* raised *its* lusty voice in unison. (Singular entity)

The huge *flock* of Canadian geese returned to *its* winter roosting grounds. (Singular entity)

The *Board* of Trustees have settled *their* differences and no longer argue internally. (Plural entities)

The *nation* of Cherokees have expressed *their* various degrees of guilt. (Plural entities)

19 PRONOUN REFERENCE

Some writers fall into the careless habit of using *global* pronouns, that is, pronouns like *this, which,* or *it* that refer to a general idea or statement that might have been implied in previous writing. Be sure any pronoun you use refers to a specific noun or other pronoun rather than to general or suggested antecedents.

19A Be sure to use the pronouns *this, that, which,* and *it* with clearly determined, specific antecedents rather than vague, broad references to ideas stated in previous sentences, paragraphs, or chapters

VAGUE REFERENCE:

The profits the college made from the rodeo were large, *which* the faculty knew about almost immediately.

CLEAR:

The faculty knew immediately that the profits from the rodeo were large. (The pronoun is eliminated entirely).

CLEAR:

> The profits the college made from the rodeo were large, an observation which the faculty made almost immediately. (A specific antecedent [observation] is created for the pronoun *which*).

VAGUE REFERENCE:

> He was fair, and he went out of his way to help his students by keeping extensive office hours and by conducting long tutorial sessions on his own time. *This* made him very popular.

CLEAR:

> He was popular because he was fair, and he went out of his way to help his students by keeping extensive office hours and by conducting long tutorial sessions on his own time. (The pronoun is eliminated entirely).

CLEAR:

> His being fair and going out of his way to help his students made him very popular. (The pronoun is eliminated entirely).

VAGUE REFERENCE:

> The government finally enacted changes in the capital gains tax, but *it* took time.

CLEAR:

> The government finally enacted changes in the capital gains tax, but such legislation took time. (The pronoun is eliminated entirely).

CLEAR:

> The government's finally enacting changes in the capital gains tax took time. (The pronoun is eliminated entirely).

19B Avoid sentences in which there are two or more possible antecedents for a pronoun

AMBIGUOUS REFERENCE:

> Logan told Smith that he was a crook. (Does *he* refer to Logan or Smith?)

CLEAR:

> Logan said to Smith, "You are a crook."

CLEAR:

> Logan said to Smith, "I am a crook."

CLEAR:

> Logan admitted to Smith that he was a crook.

CLEAR:

> Logan accused Smith of being a crook.

AMBIGUOUS REFERENCE:

> My children collected so many aluminum cans that I got rid of them. (Does *them* refer to the children or the cans?)

Note: The fact that it is common sense that the writer discarded the cans rather than the children does not reduce the ambiguity. The reader still has to make a choice he or she should not be required to make.

CLEAR:

> I got rid of the aluminum cans that my children collected.

19C Avoid references to inaccessible or distant antecedents

INACCESSIBLE:

> The law books are housed in a gleaming new library with electronic retrieval chutes, personal elevators to the ten stack levels, and student aides who will fetch and carry for all the visiting scholars. *They* are color coded according to function. (The pronoun *they* is too far removed from its antecedent *books*).

INACCESSIBLE:

> Flocks of Canada Geese gathered on the old farm in the midst of the bright reds, oranges, and yellows that marked the arrival of autumn. *They* were usually grouped in gaggles of nine or ten. (The pronoun *they* is too far removed from its antecedent *flocks*).

19D Be careful to use the relative pronoun *who, which,* and *that* for suitable antecedents

Always use the relative pronoun *who* to refer to persons and, sometimes, close family pets or named animals.

> Mayberry is the police officer *who* walks the beat in Reseda.

> The woman *who* started the feminist movement became very bitter.

> Lassie is the collie *who* crossed a continent to find her owner.

The pronoun *which* is generally used to refer to animals and things.

> The Los Angeles River, *which* is almost always dry, can become fierce and deadly during the rainy season.

The pronoun *that* refers to animals and common nouns.

> The face *that* launched a thousand ships belonged to Helen of Troy.

> The animal *that* most people fear is the boa constrictor.

The pronoun *whose* almost always refers to people, but it is occasionally used to refer to animals and things to avoid an awkward or convoluted sentence.

> The plane *whose* landing gear jammed will run out of fuel at 14:42.

> The lion *whose* mane became stuck in the gate was protesting mightily.

20 SENTENCE STRUCTURE

20A Simple sentences

A sentence is a group of words with a *subject* and *predicate* expressing *one complete thought*.

> The infant smiled.

or

> Mary fried the eggs.

The subject names the noun or pronoun doing the action or being written about, such as *Mary* in the sentence above. The predicate, *fried the eggs,* includes the verb and any of its complements or modifiers.

The simple sentence has other names: **independent clause** is the most common, although **simple clause** is frequently used. **Dependent clauses** are sentences that have been slightly altered so that they cannot stand alone (because their meaning is incomplete), but must be attached to an independent clause, where they actually act as a noun, adjective, or an adverb. Such dependent clauses are also known as **subordinate clauses.** The act of placing an idea in a dependent clause is called **subordination**.

> **Mary fried the eggs**
> Independent Clause
> *which her son had brought from the hen house.*
> Dependent Clause (Adjective Clause)

> **Mary fried the eggs**
> Independent Clause
> *when her family finally came downstairs.*
> Dependent Clause (Adverb Clause)

> **Mary knew that they all** *were very hungry.*
> Independent Clause   Dependent Clause (Noun Clause)

20B Complex sentences

Any combination of independent clauses and dependent clauses, such as the three examples above, is known as a complex sentence. It is important to keep in mind the effect and importance of subordination in writing. Subordinate clauses carry a great deal of information and meaning, and yet allow the subject and verb named in the independent clause to remain dominant and visible as the main idea.

20C Compound sentences

The compound sentence consists of at least two simple sentences joined by means of a coordinating conjunction, *and, but, for, or,* and *yet.* Independent clauses joined in this manner are given equal emphasis, a process which is called **coordination**.

> Mary fried the eggs, and she set out great slabs of hot sourdough toast.

> President Bush improved our reputation overseas, and he dispelled any doubts about American military prowess.

Again, it is important to be aware of the effect of coordination on your message. With coordination, you are giving equal emphasis to each clause and to each idea that clause communicates. Semicolons and conjunctive adverbs like *therefore, nevertheless, although, however,* yet, or *consequently* can also be used to join and coordinate clauses. Writing a succession of separate sentences is also a kind of coordination, but, without some subordination, it often results in muddied communication, the result of too many main ideas.

The three sentence structures, **simple, complex,** and **compound,** are practical tools that a thoughtful writer uses to shape his thoughts as he develops them. They complement and balance each other in the paragraph. They prevent monotony and permit refreshing combinations of ideas.

20D Basic sentence patterns

The simple sentence, while it is the basic building element in the process of writing, is really not quite so simple. Its versatility is reflected in the fact that it can assume three basic patterns:

1. PATTERN I: N V$_{INTRANSITIVE}$.
     The bully laughed.

Pattern I sentences are always built around intransitive verbs, that is, verbs that do not require a word of completion like a direct object. They give emphasis to the action of the subject. Note that the modification of the verb does not change the pattern. Other examples of Pattern I:

> **George shaves** every morning.

> **Mary studied** all through the night.

> Most **animals migrate** to warmer climates.

> **The** severe **judge** finally **smiled**.

2. PATTERN II: N V$_{TRANSITIVE}$ N$_{DIRECT OBJECT}$.
        Raul   ate   a   Big Mac.

Pattern II sentences are always built around transitive verbs, that is, verbs that do require a completer or direct object. Pattern II sentences emphasize the transfer of action from the subject to the receiver of the action, called the **direct object**. Other Pattern II sentences:

> **Elizabeth sheared the sheep.**

> **William's arrow hit the bullseye.**

> **Biff carved the turkey.**

> **Amir rejected the offer.**

3. PATTERN IIA:
   N V$_{TRANSITIVE VERB}$ N$_{INDIRECT}$ N$_{DIRECT}$
          send   OBJECT   OBJECT.
          show
          give
          tell
          make
   John   made   Piper a slingshot.

Pattern IIA is a variation of Pattern II. The sentence centers around a transitive verb, but the transitive verb is a specialized verb like *send, show, tell, give, make,* and *more.* Specialized transitive verbs like *give* permit the writer or speaker to include a secondary receiver of the action after the transitive verb and before the direct object. These secondary receivers of the action are called **indirect objects**.

> Fred made Lydia a cup of coffee.
> subject transitive indirect   direct
>   verb   object   object

June knitted her father a sweater.
subject · transitive verb · indirect object · direct object

Professor Lyle showed the students an albino anemone.
subject · transitive verb · indirect object · direct object

The store gave each patron a calendar.
subject · transitive verb · indirect object · direct object

4. PATTERN IIB:

N	V_{TRANSITIVE VERB}	N_{DIRECT OBJECT}	N_{OBJECTIVE COMPLEMENT.}
	elect		
	vote		
	appoint		
	consider		
	name		
The people	voted	Clinton	President.

Pattern IIB also is a variation of Pattern II. The sentence is still based on a transitive verb, but the transitive verb is a specialized verb like *elect, vote, appoint, consider, label, designate, name,* and others. Specialized transitive verbs like *elect* permit the writer or speaker to add a modifier of the direct object to the end of the sentence. That modifier of the direct object is called the **objective complement,** and it can be either a noun or an adjective.

Subject	Verb	Direct Object	Objective Complement
The students	considered	the course	boring. (Adj.)
The voters	elected	Wayne	sheriff. (Noun)
The police	thought	the rock show	disruptive. (Adj)
The governor	named	Michael	appellate judge. (Noun)

5. PATTERN III:

N V_{LINKING} N.   or   N V_{LINKING} Adj.

Jason is a student.   Jason is studious.

Pattern III sentences are always built around linking verbs (like *is, seems, looks, appears, feels*), that is, verbs which do not show much action, but which link nouns and adjectives to the subject in such a way that they describe or modify the subject. The words linked to the subject in this manner are called **predicate nouns** or **predicate adjectives** (they are also sometimes called **subjective complements**). Other examples of Pattern III:

Subject Predicate Adjective	Subject Predicate Noun
This **house** is nearly **new.**	**Wilma** is certainly a **beauty.**
Morris looks really **tired.**	**Donald** became a **sergeant.**
Sumo became **angry.**	**Dr. Ramsey** had been a **surgeon.**
Avalon is **tall.**	My **uncle** is a **policeman.**

20E Dependent clauses

Dependent clauses are statements that have a subject and predicate but are made subordinate to the independent clause to which they are attached. They always assume the function of a noun, adjective, or adverb, and accordingly are called a *noun clause, adjective clause,* or *adverb clause.*

A **noun clause** is a subordinate clause used as a noun. Within a sentence, it may be used as the subject, the direct object, a predicate noun, or an objective complement. Noun clauses are usually headed by one of the following words: *that, who, whoever, whom, whomever, what, whatever.* Because they are nouns, they frequently become part of the basic structure of an independent clause.

They knew **that the gun was loaded.**

Whoever rang the doorbell last night had chocolate on his fingers.

What I want for Christmas is a tool box.

An **adjective clause** is a subordinate clause used as an adjective. Within a sentence, it is usually located adjacent to the word it modifies. Adjective clauses are usually headed by one of the following words: *who, whom, whose, which, that.*

The man **who is raking the lawn** is my uncle Bill.

Jason Freund is the man **whom you saw at my house.**

Is Stanford the school **that you want to attend?**

An **adverb clause** is a subordinate clause used as an adverb. Adverb clauses are usually headed by a subordinating conjunction such as *if, unless, because, before, after, since, as.* Because they are adverbs, they are the most movable of modifiers, and can appear in various positions throughout the sentence. Remember that all adverbs, including adverb clauses, answer the questions *how, when, where,* and *why* about the verb.

Because it was so cold that night, Stan started up the main furnace.

I will give you a gold pocket watch **when you graduate from high school.**

The new police chief, **if he is wise,** will begin a neighborhood patrol program.

20F Phrases

No discussion of basic patterns and dependent clauses should leave out the third basic element of the sentence, **the phrase.** Phrases are small bundles of related words like *in the morning, of my children, brought by the storm, selling popcorn,* or *to make money.* However short and sometimes trivial they seem, they make up more than half the words of written English and provide writers and speakers with still more ways of subordinating ideas and information. Phrases usually function within a sentence as single words do, such as a noun, adjective, or adverb. On the basis of their form, they are classified as *prepositional, participial, gerund, infinitive,* and *verb* phrases. See verbals section.

PREPOSITIONAL:

She threw the ball **into the dugout.** (Adverb)

PARTICIPIAL:

The town **destroyed by the hurricane** was Homestead. (Adjective)

GERUND:

> ***Eating too much salt*** can cause a person to retain water. (Noun)

INFINITIVE:

> The employees wanted ***to buy their own company.*** (Noun)

VERB PHRASE:

> By the first of the year, all of the remodeling **will have been** completed. (Verb)

20G Sentence fragments

A sentence fragment is a part of a sentence that has been punctuated as if it were a complete sentence. It does not express a complete thought but depends upon a nearby independent clause for its full meaning. It should be made a part of that complete sentence.

INCORRECT:

> I was not able to pick up my child at her school. *Having been caught in heavy traffic.* (Participial phrase)

REVISED:

> Having been caught in heavy traffic, I was not able to pick up my child at her school.

OR

> I was not able to pick up my child at her school. I had been caught in heavy traffic.

INCORRECT:

> The cat sat on the water heater. *Unable to get warm.* (Adjective phrase)

REVISED:

> Unable to get warm, the cat sat on the water heater.

INCORRECT:

> The salesman tightened the wire around the burlap feed bag with a spinner. *Which twists wire loops until they are secure.*
> (Adjective clause)

REVISED:

> The salesman tightened the wire around the burlap feed bag with a spinner, which twists wire loops until they are secure.

INCORRECT:

> We will probably try to find another insurance company. *When our policy expires.* (Adverb clause)

REVISED:

> When our policy expires, we will probably try to find another insurance company.

20H Run-on sentences

Probably the most common error in writing occurs when two sentences are run together as one. There are two types of run-on sentences: the *fused* sentence, which has no punctuation mark between its two independent clauses, and the *comma splice*, which substitutes a comma where either a period or a semicolon is needed.

FUSED:

> Jean had no luck at the store they were out of umbrellas.

COMMA SPLICE:

> She surprised us all with her visit, she was on her way to New York.

To correct a run-on sentence, use a period, a semicolon, or a coordinating conjunction (*and, but, or, nor, for*) to separate independent clauses.

Note the following examples of run-on sentences and the suggested revisions.

FUSED:

> Eric is a bodybuilder he eats only large amounts of meat.

REVISED:

> Eric is a bodybuilder; he eats only large amounts of meat.

COMMA SPLICE:

> He had never seen Alex so prepared, he even had backup copies of his study sheets!

REVISED:

> He had never seen Alex so prepared. He even had backup copies of his study sheets!

COMMA SPLICE:

> His father was an artist, his mother was an accountant.

REVISED:

> His father was an artist and his mother was an accountant.

20I Faulty coordination or subordination

FAULTY COORDINATION:

> The real power in the company lies with Mr. Stark, and he currently owns 55 percent of the stock; in addition to that, his mother is semiretired as president of the firm.

REVISED:

> The real power in the company lies with Mr. Stark, who currently owns 55 percent of the stock and whose mother is semiretired as president of the firm.

Notice that subordinating two of the independent clauses tightens the sentence and adds focus.

Subordination of too many parts of a sentence, however, can be just as confusing. Look at the following example:

EXCESSIVE SUBORDINATION:

> Standing on the corner were many aliens who had entered the country illegally, and most of whom had applied for amnesty, and even more important to them though, who had families back in Mexico or El Salvador who needed food and shelter.

REVISED:

> Standing on the corner were many illegal aliens, most of whom had applied for amnesty. Even more important to them, though, was the fact that they had families needing food and shelter back in Mexico or El Salvador.

Notice how proper coordination and subordination helps clarify a confusing stream of excessively entwined modifiers.

You must also keep in mind the *logic* of subordination. What you choose to subordinate in a sentence has to make sense to the reader. For example, the sentence "Sue happened to glance at the sky, amazed to see an enormous flying saucer hovering over the barn" gives greater importance to the fact that Sue glanced at the sky. A more logical version of that sentence is, "Happening to glance at the sky, Sue was amazed to see an enormous flying saucer hovering over the barn."

BACKWARD SUBORDINATION:

> She studied medicine with great intensity for fifteen years, becoming a doctor.

LOGICAL REVISION:

> She became a doctor, having studied medicine with great intensity for fifteen years.

BACKWARD SUBORDINATION:

> The pitcher momentarily let the runner on first base take a wide lead, when he stole second.

LOGICAL REVISION:

> The runner stole second when the pitcher momentarily let him take a wide lead.

BACKWARD SUBORDINATION:

> He ran over with a fire extinguisher, saving the driver's life.

LOGICAL REVISION:

> Running over with a fire extinguisher, he saved the driver's life.

21   PREDICATION

21A   **Predication refers to the process of joining the *naming* part of the sentence (the *subject*) to the *doing* or *describing* part of the sentence (the *predicate*)**

Subject	Predicate
People	are buying more fish.
Celia	is a counselor.

It is not likely that a writer or reader will have trouble linking the subjects and predicates of sentences as short as these. It is in the use of longer, more detailed sentences that predication errors come about. Illogical predication equates unlike constructions and ideas. Look at the following incorrect examples.

INCORRECT:

> By working at such technical plants as Lockheed and Bendix gives the engineering students insight into what will be expected of them. (*By working* does not give them insight; *working* does.)

> According to one authority, the ages of thirty to forty are subject to the most pressures concerning self-identity. (The *ages* are not subject to the pressures, but rather the *people* of those ages.)

> The sheer simplicity of frozen food may soon replace home-cooked meals. (*Simplicity* will not replace the meals; *frozen food* will, *because* of its simplicity of preparation.)

> Paying bills on time causes many worries for young families. (*Paying* bills does not cause worries, but *not paying* them does.)

21B   ***Is when, is where, is because***

The use of *is when, is where, is because* is always incorrect. The reason is simple: *when, where,* and *because* introduce adverbial clauses; and a noun subject followed by a form of the verb *to be* must be equated with a noun structure, not with an adverb clause.

INCORRECT:

> Lepidopterology is where you study butterflies and moths.

CORRECT:

> Lepidopterology is the study of butterflies and moths. (Here, the adverb clause *where you study...* has been changed to a subject complement: *lepidopterology = study.*)

INCORRECT:

> The reason they won is because they had better coaching.

CORRECT:

> The reason they won is that they had better coaching. (The noun clause *that they had better coaching* equates with the noun *reason.*)

OR

> They won because they had better coaching. (The adverb clause modifies the verb *won.*)

21C   **Parallelism**

Parallel ideas in a sentence should be expressed in the same grammatical form. If they are not, the sentence will be unbalanced.

1. A series of coordinated elements should be parallel in form.

INCORRECT:

He enjoys *plays, exhibitions,* and *to walk* every morning. (An infinitive is paired with two nouns.)

CORRECT:

He enjoys *going* to plays, *visiting* exhibitions, and *walking* every morning.

OR

He enjoys *plays, exhibitions,* and morning *walks.*

INCORRECT:

The union wanted *pay increases for every employee and that there would be shorter working hours.* (A noun is paired with a noun clause.)

CORRECT:

The union wanted *pay increases* for every employee and shorter *working hours.*

2. The constructions that follow correlative conjunctions *(both-and, either-or, neither-nor, not only-but also, whether-or)* should be parallel in form.

INCORRECT:

He was neither qualified to lead this country nor was he willing.

CORRECT:

He was neither qualified nor willing to lead this country.

3. Do not use *and* before *which* or *who* unless the sentence has a previously expressed *which* or *who* clause with which to be parallel.

INCORRECT:

She is a well-known surgeon from New York, and who has written many books on brain surgery.

CORRECT:

She is a well-known surgeon from New York, who has lectured at many medical schools and who has written many books on brain surgery.

NOTE:

A sentence may lack parallelism even though its parts are *grammatically* parallel. If the ideas are not logically equal, then the flow of ideas is not parallel.

INCORRECT:

The dean introduced new faculty members, explained some curriculum strategies, began an exploratory discussion of the accreditation process, *spilled coffee on his tie,* reviewed the budget for the fiscal year, and *went to lunch with Don Love.* (Although the italicized phrases are grammatically parallel, they are not parallel with the other ideas expressed.)

22 TRANSITIONAL WORDS AND PHRASES

22A Words of transition are clues that help the reader to follow the writer's flow of ideas

Confusion can result, however, when an illogical or incorrect connective is used. The following list includes more commonly used transitional words and phrases, and the concepts they suggest.

ADDITION:

also, furthermore, moreover, similarly, too, in addition.

Besides the evacuation of patients, moreover, we need to think of supplies.

CAUSE AND EFFECT:

accordingly, as a result, consequently, hence, so, therefore, thus

As a result, the dam burst and flooded ten square miles of rich farmland.

CONCESSION:

granted that, it is true that, no doubt, to be sure

To be sure, neither side wanted a war.

CONCLUSION:

in short, that is, to conclude, to sum up

In short, after the agreement was reached, the parties lived in peace.

CONTRAST:

although, but, however, nevertheless, on the contrary, on the other hand

On the contrary, few members of the audience were displeased with the show.

EXAMPLE:

for example, for instance

For instance, one motorist stopped his car and refused to move.

22B Watch for errors in logical use of transitional words

INCORRECT:

At many gas stations, drivers have to pump their own gasoline; *therefore,* at Ken's Union Station, full service is still the rule.

CORRECT:

At many gas stations, drivers have to pump their own gasoline; *however* at Ken's Union Station, full service is still the rule.

23 STRATEGY/WRITING STRATEGIES

Once you as a writer complete a paragraph or essay, and have carefully proofread your work, you still need to give it one more overall evaluation. You must make sure you have selected the most logical transitions between paragraphs, and have used language that is appropriate for the intended audience. You should check whether or not you have added enough supporting material to adequately complete each paragraph, and whether or not every sentence or paragraph is relevant to the selection. A good way to prepare for a final review is to become familiar with basic writing strategies and some of the principles that apply to each.

23A Description

Descriptive writing usually relies on sense impressions—records of what the eye sees, the ear hears, the nose smells, the tongue tastes, and the skin feels. If you are contemplating how a descriptive selection can be strengthened, be sure to consider the addition of more specific sense impressions.

In addition to sense impressions, descriptive writing often employs a *dominant impression* at the outset of the selection, a controlling idea that helps unify the passage and place the specific details employed.

> Smith was a great bear of a man, and, when he stooped through the frame of a door, he virtually filled the opening. Once he made it through and stood at his full height again, he sort of reared up, exactly like a bear facing an intruder. Nor was he much more friendly. Framed by matted, curly red hair, his wide face communicated a perpetual scowl, intensified by large, stark, wide-set blue eyes that expressed unrelenting outrage at what they saw. Beneath the eyes, high, weathered cheekbones gave his face its Slavic expanse, and his large flat nose was misshapen by decades of bar brawls. His vast, red handlebar mustache accented the large twisted lips that expressed grim displeasure; and beneath, his huge chin stuck out like a battering ram.

23B Narration

Narration is usually a series of events presented in chronological sequence, all of which have one purpose: *to tell what happened*. Narration, primarily used in story-telling, biographical histories, diaries, and journals, is a fundamental strategy in all writing. To be effective, narration requires coherent order and also a good deal of rich, descriptive detail.

Any discussion of the structure of the narrative passage focuses on the order of events that make up the narrative. The exact chronological relationships among the events are signaled by tenses, transitions, and time markers. Notice how the author of the following selection uses each of these cues to establish coherent order.

In the past, this type of literature—whether in books or magazines—was published under such titles as *Travel Adventures, Wonder Stories, Fantastic Tales* or *Mysteries of the Universe*. It took garish "headlines" like these to draw attention to the special nature of this material.

In 1929, Hugo Gernsback, a New York magazine publisher and one of the great pioneers in the field we are exploring here, provided the much-needed common denominator by coining the inspired term *science fiction*.

Instantly and universally, science fiction was defined and accepted as a form of literature distinct and apart from all others, a form that imposed on the writer none of the shackles that confine traditional writing to the limits of so many rules and precedents.

Comfortably settled under the aegis of its brand-new generic name, science fiction prospered in spite of a worldwide depression and World War II. Other entertainment media contributed their share. The movies gave us Boris Karloff as Frankenstein's monster and Fredric March as Dr. Jekyll. In 1938, a science fiction radio program about Martian invaders threw the East Coast of the United States into a panic.

Note that the events in the development of science fiction are carefully presented in a clear, coherent sequence and include cues that leave no doubt about the order in which these events took place. For instance, the use of *in the past this type of literature . . . was published* in the first paragraph establishes the fact that science fiction existed in some form before the events described in the subsequent paragraphs. In the next three paragraphs, such transitions and time markers as *in 1929, instantly* and *universally, comfortably settled...under...brand-new...name, worldwide depression, World War II*, and *in 1938* firmly establish the relative order of events.

23C Explanation of a process

Explaining a process is, in some ways, similar to narration; however, you have to be even more careful with the sequence of events. Narration adheres *in general* to a sequence; a process depends *exactly* on a sequence, one that can be repeated time after time with the same results. In explaining a process, the use of transitional signals such as *after, before, next, immediately, while the [glue] is still [wet]*, and *when [this] is done*, to indicate the sequence of steps, is an essential writing strategy. To evaluate the sequence of steps in a process passage, pay careful attention to transitional words and phrases.

23D Classification and division

Classification helps organize detailed material into different groups so that it can be dealt with in steps or stages, can be seen more clearly, or can be explained or illustrated in all its diversity.

Suppose that you are a newspaper writer who specializes in communicable diseases and that you want to do an article on major diseases that still plague our society today. You might divide the diseases in the following way:

COMMUNICABLE DISEASES VIRULENT TODAY

Viruses	Bacteria	Fungi	Protozoa	Worms
Chicken Pox	Pneumonia	Athlete's	Amebic	Flukes
Measles	Botulism	Foot	Dystentery	Tapeworms
Mumps	Tetanus	Ringworm	Malaria	Hookworms
Influenza	Gonorrhea		Sleeping	Pinworms
Polio	Tuberculosis		Sickness	Trichinal
Hepatitis				Worms
Rabies				
AIDS				

Each division and subdivision of a subject must make sense, that is, it must be necessary for the writer's purpose and also understandable to the reader. The division must be based upon some clear principle: in the diagram of communicable diseases, for instance, each disease type heads a category. The actual diseases form the subdivisions in each category.

23E Definition

A definition usually takes the form of one or more paragraphs within a larger piece of writing. The writer has decided at that point in the essay that an explanation is needed of the nature or essential qualities of something.

A definition begins by placing the term being defined into *a class;* then it lists the details by which the term can be *distinguished* from other members of that class. For example, a blender is in the class of small kitchen appliances; it can be distinguished from other members of that class—like toasters, can openers, and waffle irons—by the fact that it blends liquids. Here are some other examples:

Term Being Defined	Class to Which It Belongs	Distinguishing Characteristics
A stove is	a kitchen appliance	designed to heat and cook food.
Freedom is	a political condition	without restraints or limitations.
A lion is	a feline animal	that inhabits wide plains areas.
Psychiatry is	the medical field	dealing with physical and behavioral disorders of the mind.

An extended definition begins with this simple form and builds upon it, using any of the techniques common to other strategies.

23F Comparison and contrast

A common way to explain something is to show how it is *similar to* or *different from* something else—in other words, to *compare* or *contrast*. You have two main options in comparing and contrasting: (a) you can present the similarities or differences point by point, turning first to one subject and then to the other each time, or (b) you can treat each subject as a whole, finishing with one during the first half of the essay, and then with the other.

In either case, strict organization of the specific differences and similarities between one item and the other is essential. In addition, there has to be some balance and some sense of equal treatment of each subject to establish coherence.

23G Cause and effect

Cause-and-effect essays can be immensely complicated and, as a result, require more careful organization than any other strategic approach. The cause-and-effect essay or paragraph usually begins with a clear, detailed examination of the *effect* that is the essay subject (such as the slow death of Monterey pine trees around Lake Arrowhead in Southern California) and then proceeds to discuss each of the causes in detail, usually in order of importance.

What can be more troublesome about cause-and-effect essays is that both causes and effects are usually multiple; there are frequently not only several causes, but also primary *and* secondary effects as well. What is more, there is a progression of importance among the causes.

23H Persuasion

For our purposes, the term *persuasion* refers to either argument (usually defined as an appeal to logic) or persuasion (defined as an appeal to emotion or ethics). In a persuasion paper, the writer hopes to *convince* the reader and attempts to do so through a series of steps: (1) gain the reader's attention, (2) outline the problem or situation, (3) anticipate or recognize opposing points of view, and (4) appeal to both reason and emotion (in the choice of examples and details).

24 HOW TO WRITE AN IMPROMPTU ESSAY

On-the-spot essays differ considerably from the papers you write at home, revise and proofread several times, and then turn in to your professor. In fact, by the time you write your final version of an at-home paper, you are actually *rewriting* it, going back to be sure it meets the basic standards of an essay:

I. A clearly evident, three-part structure.

   A. An **Introduction** that gives a general answer to the question posed as well as a skeletal plan of the whole paper;

   B. A **Body** that strengthens or develops the answer, providing details and supporting points that develop the plan blocked out in the introduction;

   C. A **Conclusion** that brings the essay to a close by restating your main points or concluding in some other way.

II. A comprehensive, complete treatment of the subject, with many concrete supporting details.

III. A well-written paper that presents one distinct idea.

IV. A paper free of writing errors.

These standards are quite difficult to meet if you are writing an in-class, timed essay; fortunately, you can be sure that the professors who grade the papers know that. They <u>do</u> expect you to have a rough structure, however, a **beginning,** a **middle,** and an **end.** They expect your paper to have unity, meaning a distinct idea to which everything logically relates, as well as **coherence,** a logical and understandable flow of ideas. In other words, they expect a straightforward, sharp, detailed **statement** from you. In many ways, the on-the-spot essay that you are expected to write is more like a speech than the formal at-home essay, and it is unlikely your professors will grade you down if you are somewhat informal and conversational in writing it.

24A Where do I begin?

Many students who take timed writing tests tend to be a little nervous, and begin writing without first planning their essay. Once you are given your subject, you need to plan and think a little, and should not consider it wasted time. In fact, anticipate five to eight minutes of preparation time before you write, during which you will be writing a pregnant sentence and its supporting points.

24B Pregnant sentences

The main idea of your essay must be expressed in one sentence. It must be a sentence, because only a sentence is able to express an **idea,** and it is the **idea** that you will be developing in your essay. Once you write your **pregnant sentence,** everything you write must flow derivatively from it, and from it alone.

Take the following assignment:

> "The best things in life are free." In a busy world like ours, people tend to overlook the value of commonplace objects, relationships, pets, possessions, or other aspects of life. Write a well-organized essay about something that you consider very valuable though it is usually taken for granted. Be sure to explain in detail why you believe your subject is valuable.

One of my students, Lisa, likes dogs and knows a little about them. When she read the question, she decided to try dogs as a subject. First, she had to transform the topic into a pregnant sentence so that her essay would have an underlying idea. She thought for awhile, and then scribbled on a scrap of paper:

> Dogs...what value?
>
> What do they do for us?
>
>   -police dogs
>
> -guide dogs
>
>   -sniffers
>
> -protect our homes
>
>   -companions and pets
>
>   -save lives

At this point, Lisa was ready to write her pregnant sentence.

> Dogs are a valuable asset to our society.

She then performed the "content" test by asking, **"how or in what way"** are dogs a valuable asset to our society? Here is what she came up with.

1. They can be taught to perform jobs.

2. They protect you and your property.

3. They give pleasure and companionship.

There seems a good deal to say about the pregnant sentence **Dogs are a valuable asset to our society.** Notice that each sentence **directly** answers the test question. There are no sentences that are vaguely and aimlessly related to the pregnant sentence like, "I had a miniature collie once," or "Dogs differ from cats in their attentiveness to their owners."

Lisa also thought of the following sentences:

4. They are employed in extensive medical research.

5. Breeding and showing dogs is a significant business.

These two sentences do meet the test. They answer the question, **"How or in what way are dogs a valuable asset to our society?"**

However, she decided that they were a trifle off topic, because they differ from the others in the impersonal way the dogs are treated in research and breeding. She kept them in mind, anyway, in case she ran a little short later on. The next step for Lisa was to write three or so sentences **that are directly derived from** each of the second-level sentences. Again, it is very important that you write **sentences** so that you remain in the realm of **ideas,** not topics. And again, it is very important that each of these second-level sentences do not wander away from the idea being developed.

> Dogs are a valuable asset to our society.
>
> 1. They can be taught to perform jobs.
>
>   A. Dogs are trained to be police dogs and professional watch dogs.
>
>   B. Dogs are used to assist the handicapped.
>
>   C. Dogs are used to detect drugs and explosives.
>
> 2. They protect you and your property.
>
>   A. Barking dogs will usually deter an intruder from entering your home.
>
>   B. Dogs will alert you of a presence near their home.
>
>   C. If a stranger enters a person's home, many dogs will act aggressively toward the intruder.
>
> 3. Dogs are loyal companions.
>
>   A. Dogs have given their lives to protect police officers.

B. Dogs remain faithful to their friend regardless of the treatment they are given.

C. Dogs truly are man's best friend.

While she was jotting down this little outline, Lisa was accomplishing two essential preparatory tasks: first, she was planning her entire essay, and second, she was checking to see if her pregnant sentence/topic had enough substance to be developed into a full essay. It may seem a time-consuming exercise, but notice that her essay is all but written now. As she wrote the essay, Lisa made several impromptu additions and changes, as you will see in the following versions.

Lisa's essay:

The Value of Dogs to Society.

The term "dumb animal" perplexes me, especially when it is applied to our canine friends. I have always considered dogs a valuable asset to society. They are trained to perform jobs to assist man, they protect their owners and their owner's possessions, and they are great companions. I strongly believe that dogs are a valuable asset to society and that a world without dogs would be a lesser place.

The jobs that dogs perform to assist their masters are often important jobs, such as police work. When the day is done, these same dogs are the family pet, gentle and loving to children and other family members. Who can discredit dogs that are the eyes of the blind or the ears of the deaf? Consider airport customs dogs who detect drugs. In return for such valuable work, a dog requires little.

After writing this paragraph, Lisa felt she had a good start. She had established a distinct idea in the first paragraph, and written one of the three supporting paragraphs that will comprise the middle or generative part of her essay. Something was not right, however. Lisa realized that she was not developing enough of a statement, and that the work she was writing would sound sparse and abbreviated, a chronic problem she has had with her writing throughout her years in school. However, she had to be careful at this point. If she added sentences carelessly, she would destroy the unity of her essay, that is, the unimpeded and undeviated flow of specific details that strengthens and enriches the single idea declared in the pregnant sentence, **Dogs are an asset to society.** To avoid disturbing the unity she had achieved, she decided to rewrite her second paragraph, building it **from the inside,** that is generating content by becoming more specific about what she had already written, making the idea more clear and meaningful rather than adding new and competing ideas.

Here is her final version. The italicized portions of the second paragraph are what she added. As she wrote the rest of the essay, she continued to add layers of concrete and specific modification to her sentences.

The Value of Dogs to Society.

The term "dumb animal" perplexes me, especially when it is applied to our canine friends. I have always considered dogs a valuable asset to society. They are trained to perform jobs to assist man, they protect their owners and their owner's possessions, and they are great companions. I strongly believe that dogs are a valuable asset to society and that a world without dogs would be a lesser place.

The jobs that dogs perform to assist their masters are often important jobs, such as police work, *search and rescue duty, and the control of herd animals. Possessing a keen sense of duty, police dogs function as partners to police officers, and frequently find and subdue armed criminals. In addition, if an officer is ever confronted by a threatening or unruly group of people, a police dog can keep them at a distance. Yet,* when the day is done, these same dogs are the family pet, gentle and loving to children and other family members. Who can discredit dogs that are the eyes of the blind or the ears of the deaf? Consider airport customs dogs who, *employing their vastly superior sense of smell,* detect drugs *and explosives in mountains of luggage.* In return for such valuable work, a dog requires *nothing more than some kibbles and a scratch under the ears or a "Good dog!"*

Even in the ways we entertain ourselves, dogs play a significant role. When I lived in New York, I used to attend Greyhound races with my father and uncle in Flushing. What a thrill it was to walk through the prep areas, choose a dog I thought was going to win, and then see him whip over the finish line a body length ahead of his competitors. In racing one really sees the difference breeding can make in the development of a dog, most of the winners being related to past champions. Breeding also figures importantly in the blood lines of hunting dogs and show dogs.

How many of us know of people, perhaps elderly people, who live with a dog and consider the dogs a stable and positive part of their lives? Many studies have proven that dogs have beneficial effects upon the health or feelings of well being of their elderly owners. Their beneficial effects range from lowering the heart rate of their owners to giving them a purpose for living. Dogs in such circumstances are saving lives as surely as the legendary Saint Bernard who traveled frigid alpine trails with a cask of rum under his neck.

Personally, I feel safe in my own home, knowing my Labrador will alert me to an unknown intruder, and that an unknown intruder will be wary of my Labrador. Instinctively territorial in nature, it's no wonder dogs make such effective guards.

The loyalty of this animal astounds me. Every day, police dogs risk their lives to maintain the safety of their human partners. This loyalty is not reserved for loving masters either. A dog will love you regardless of ill treatment, abuse, or neglect. I know I do not stand alone in my one-sided opinion of dogs. Somewhere along the line someone called dogs "man's best friend." I am inclined to agree.

24C Writing assignments

Number	Topic	Length P=Paragraph E=Essay
1	Write a paragraph describing a scene with which you are familiar, a view of your school, your favorite vacation spot, a kitchen you feel comfortable in, a workshop, a holiday table setting, or a distinctive bedroom.	P:200 wrds E:300-500
2	Describe or discuss something that frightens you now, or did when you were a child.	P:200 E:300-500
3	Define an abstract term in a well-developed paragraph. Examples of abstract terms: honesty, enthusiasm, love, commitment, prejudice, poverty.	P:200 E:250-300
4	Write a paragraph in which you describe the qualifications for a job or occupation.	P:250-300
5	Compare and contrast two people, places, or objects.	P:250-300 E:300-500
6	Write a process essay in which you clearly set forth the materials, tools, and steps in completing a project. Example topics are writing an excellent essay, painting a car, trimming a tree, binding a book, or washing a cat.	E:300-500
7	Discuss an experience in which you or someone you know was excluded from a group.	P:250-300 E:300-400
8	Write a well organized paragraph or short essay in which you explain how man has used the forces of nature to his benefit.	P:250 E:300-500
9	Compare and contrast two very different time frames in your life.	P:250-300 E:300-500
10	Discuss an issue in your school or present circumstances that you believe should be changed. Describe the change you would like to see, and explain how it would bring about an improvement.	P:200-250 E:300-500
11	Explain what you believe to be ethical behavior in the classroom.	P:200-250 E:300-400

Number	Topic	Length P=Paragraph E=Essay
12	Look up one word in the OED. Using the information you find there, write a short history of the word.	P:200-250 E:300-400
13	Argue for a global change you would like to see made by the year 2005.	P:200-300 E:300-500
14	Write a short essay on three or four objects you own that recall specific people or events. Discuss the objects themselves and the people associated with them.	P:250-300 E:300-400
15	Discuss what you consider to be some distinguishing traits or attributes of your own ethnic or cultural background, illustrating your essay with specific details. Or, if you feel qualified, compare and contrast the characteristics of two ethnic or cultural groups.	P:200-300 E:300-450
16	Social scientists frequently cite what they see as a serious increase in violence and violent crime in recent years. What do you see as one important cause of this increased violence, and what do you think we can do to eliminate this cause?	P:250-300 E:300-400
17	Many people do poorly in their job or in school because they simply are not able to manage their time effectively. Many students are faced with the need to find time for family and jobs as well as study and leisure. How well do you do at this life management skill in order to have enough time for your studies? Explain.	P:250 E:300-500
18	Although friends are usually different from one another, there are most likely some qualities that you require of all your friends. Discuss several of these qualities, and explain why they are valuable to you.	P:250-300 E:300-500
19.	Write a paper that seems to say one thing but that actually says the opposite. That is, use an ironic voice; do not merely describe an ironic situation.	P:200-250 E:300-500
20.	Do you enjoy strolling the streets? Have you developed a pastime to keep you alert and entertained while strolling? Write an essay on your own "street pastime." What do you see or hear as you hike the streets (city or country)?	P:200-250 E:300-500

25 ORGANIZATION

25A Main idea

If a passage of prose can be viewed as soup stock and boiled in a pan until just one cup of liquid is left, that one cup can be considered the *essence* or *main idea* of that passage. It is essential to realize that every piece of writing that has real substance begins as one *main idea* from which the entire work, no matter how large or small, is derived.

For example, a passage might be about exercise (the *topic*). But what does it state about exercise? If the selection points out that exercise makes a person more alert, more fit, more productive, and more likely to live longer, the central idea is probably something like "Exercise is essential to a healthy, productive life." On the other hand, if the passage contains statements about bruised heel bones, pulled hamstrings, shinsplints, and muscle pain, then the main idea might be something similar to "Exercise can do more harm than good."

Whatever sentence you decide expresses the main idea of the passage, you must test it to make sure it really does represent the thrust of the entire selection. For example, you can ask, "In what way can exercise do more harm than good?" Or, "In what way is exercise essential to a healthy, productive life?" If every sentence and paragraph in the passage pertains to the main idea you have chosen, then you know your choice is sound. However, if you find that the passage contains sentences and paragraphs that support other ideas, then you need to start over and formulate another main idea.

Questions that test your ability to determine the central idea can be expressed in a number of ways:

The main point the author makes is. . .

The author seems chiefly concerned with. . .

The main idea of this passage is. . .

Which of the following titles could best be used for this selection?

Which of these statements best expresses the idea of the passage?

25B Supporting material

The supporting material that makes up the larger portion of most selections (often called the *body of the writing*) contains the essential material of the work—specific details, anecdotes, allusions, references, or reasons—by which a writer substantiates the main thought.

Keep in mind that supporting material may vary considerably from one context to another. The specific details in a report on a scientific discovery, for example, may be very different from the kind of detail needed in a biographical selection.

Try to be continually mindful of the logical order of paragraphs within a selection, and of the logical order of sentences within each paragraph. Transitional words and phrases usually highlight paragraph or essay coherence.

When you consider whether or not your selection is compatible with the audience or readers you intended, check the relative quality and sophistication of the supporting details. For example, a selection intended for children would probably include simple explanations and supporting details that would be unnecessary or inappropriate for adult readers. For other examples, see How to Write an Impromptu Essay, section 24.

25C Transition

Transitional words and phrases make clear the relationship between phrases, clauses, and sentences, and lend coherence to the sequence of paragraphs.

A transitional paragraph is used to link the main parts of an essay. Such a paragraph may be just a single sentence that eases the progression from one idea to the next:

EXAMPLE:

> Sometimes a solution is based upon a study of the past. Let us review what has taken place in new architecture so far this century.

Most of the time, however, transitions are individual words or phrases that provide transition while signaling a concept like addition, contrast, example, or time. The following list will show you the functions of some transitions.

Concepts	Transitions
Addition and continuation	also, and, another, besides, finally, likewise, furthermore, in addition, indeed, moreover, similarly, then, too
Cause and effect	accordingly, as, as a result, because, consequently, for this reason, since, then, therefore, thus
Concession	certainly, granted that, it is true that, no doubt, of course, still, to be sure
Conclusion or repetition	in other words, in particular, in short, In summary, once again, that is, to repeat
Contrast or limitation	although, but, however, if, in contrast, instead, nevertheless, on the contrary, on the other hand, otherwise, provided that, still, yet
Example	for example, for instance, in particular, likewise, specifically, that is, to illustrate
Place	above, behind, below, elsewhere, here, in back of, north of, on this side, there, to the right of, underneath
Time	afterward, before, earlier, eventually, immediately, later, meanwhile, next, now, since, soon, until

25D Openings and closings

The *opening paragraph* is crucial in any written communication. In a few words, the author must make clear the central purpose of the work and also convince the readers that they should continue. Sometimes, an author will use the opening paragraph to establish his or her authority for the task or to create a question in the readers' minds that they need or hope to have answered—by continuing to read.

> The land that became the United States was in colonial times an extension of the Old World into the New. Through the centuries, the descendants of the original colonists blended their European heritage into the new Nation that evolved. But for the courage and resourcefulness of the Europeans who first explored and settled the unknown wilderness, that evolution would not have been possible.

The simplest *closing paragraphs* summarize the gist of the entire passage in a sentence or two. Others invite or challenge the reader to engage in further research on the topic. A good concluding paragraph will complete the passage logically and clearly, leaving the reader with the certainty that the main idea has been adequately developed.

> The amalgamation of such rich and diverse national, cultural, and racial elements into a free and democratic society has created the United States of America—a blending of cultures, languages, and traditions that mirrors the hopes and aspirations of all mankind.

26 STYLE

A fundamental principle of writing is that style should remain consistent throughout any writing selection. If there is an obvious shift in style, the selection immediately becomes awkward and not credible to the reader.

There are several levels of formality in the prose that most students encounter: formal, informal, popular, elevated, and esoteric.

26A Formal writing style

Formal style is characterized by long and complex sentences, a scholarly vocabulary, and a consistently serious tone. Grammatical rules are scrupulously observed, and the subject matter is substantial. The selection may include references to literary works or allusions to historical and classical figures. Absent are contractions, colloquial expressions, and an identified speaker, with the impersonal *one* or *the reader* frequently used as the subject.

> The California coast, endowed with a wonderful climate and peopled by docile Indians, was ideally suited for the pastoral mission system by which New Spain had been slowly extending her northern frontiers. Elsewhere in the present United States the system had either failed or met with only moderate success; in California it thrived and reached perfection. Nevertheless, California was the last area in the United States to be penetrated by Spain—and not until the frontier lay virtually dormant elsewhere. Located as it was so far out on the lifelines of the Spanish Empire in the New World, California was sparsely populated and neglected.
>
> *Explorers and Settlers,* Government Printing Office

A formal writing style is used in serious essays, research papers, and legal documentation.

26B Informal writing style

Informal style uses the language of everyday speech, characterized by contractions, colloquialisms, and occasional slang. The topics are often light, and the approach, or tone, is conversational. Sentences are usually uncomplicated, and the writer makes no attempt to distance himself from the reader, frequently using *I* or *we* as the subject.

> Animals talk to each other, of course. There can be no question about that; but I suppose there are very few people who can understand them. I never knew but one man who could. . .This was Jim Baker. According to Jim Baker, some animals have only a limited education, and use only very simple words, and scarcely ever a comparison or a flowery figure; whereas, certain other animals have a large vocabulary, a fine command of language and a ready and fluent delivery; consequently these latter talk a great deal; they like it; they are conscious of their talent, and they enjoy "showing off."
>
> Mark Twain, *A Tramp Abroad*

26C Popular writing style

The popular style is the writing style most students use in school work. Less colloquial and relaxed than the informal, the popular style consists of longer sentences, with no contractions but some colloquialisms when necessary for clarity and immediacy. Usually the tone of the work is serious, and the content is substantial and informative. The popular style is characteristic of the language used in newspapers, magazines, and contemporary literature. Look at the following student essay, written in popular style.

> Fishing has always been an art form to the practitioner of the sport. The techniques involved in outsmarting fish are passed down from generation to generation. Sometimes this information is related in the form of direct instruction or through the use of illustrated books, but most neophytes learn by watching others fish or by being asked to "mind my pole." That is usually the time when the best fish of the day is caught. Such an occurrence can and does drive expert anglers to distraction, causing them to mutter under their breath and cast sidelong glances at a youngster who is doing everything wrong but still manages to bring in a whopper.

26D Elevated writing style

The elevated style is poetic in tone and is intended for certain solemn occasions that exist infrequently today—

for example, addressing a king or memorializing a national hero. Heightened funeral orations or eulogies now seem inappropriate, most expressions of grief or commemoration being couched in more popular styles. Literary allusions, biblical phrases, figures of speech, ornate language, gravity of tone—all are characteristic of the elevated style. The following excerpt is from a eulogy that appeared in a July 1852 newspaper.

> Alas! who can realize that Henry Clay is dead! Who can realize that never again that majestic form shall rise in the council- chambers of his country to beat back the storms of anarchy which may threaten, or pour the oil of peace upon the troubled billows as they rage and menace around?

26E Esoteric writing style

The word *esoteric* refers to knowledge that is limited to a small group. This writing style uses technical or specialized phraseology (sometimes referred to as jargon) characteristic of a particular profession, trade, or branch of learning. Groups employing such language include medical personnel, astronauts, air traffic controllers, jazz musicians, and a variety of others. The following excerpt is from a medical journal.

> Morphologic changes in the myocardium are caused by coronary obstruction leading to infarction and hemorrhaging within the wall of the sclerotic coronary vessel.

27 WORD CHOICE

27A Diction

One of the skills you need to exercise frequently in writing is to determine the appropriateness of a word in its context. In a technical passage about the development of the transistor, for example, the use of a flowery or ornate word or phrase would stand out as inappropriate. Similarly, words that are illiterate or colloquial, or used in spoken English, for the most part, are not appropriate in a formal literary passage.

A word is *appropriate* if it fits the reader, occasion, and purpose for which the writing is intended. In general, most language can be categorized as either formal, informal (colloquial), or popular.

1. Formal Diction

Formal diction is seldom used in everyday conversation and writing. It is found in writing that serves a serious purpose (for example, a research paper) and concerns weighty or substantial topics, such as death, crime, philosophy, scholarship, science, and literature.

Formal language employs a more scholarly vocabulary than popular English (*eccentric* for *strange*, *extenuation* for *excuse*, *immaculate* for *clean*, *tantamount* for *equivalent*, and so on). Another characteristic is grammatical exactness.

The following expressions have no place in formal prose.

Cool it.	yeah
guys	turn-on
high (intoxicated)	guts
spaced-out (on drugs)	I've had it!
for sure	stuck-up
creep (obnoxious person)	an awful lot
macho	screwball
rad or radical	wasted

2. Informal Diction

Informal diction is *colloquial* language, that is, the language of everyday conversation. It includes contractions (always improper in formal writing), slang, colloquialisms, dialect, and turns of phrase peculiar to local areas (*provincialisms*) and shortened word forms (*TV* for *television*, *phone* for *telephone*, *stereo* for *stereophonic set*, and so on).

3. Popular Diction

Popular diction lies somewhere between formal and informal (colloquial) diction. It is not as free as colloquial, nor does it include slang or provincialisms, but it relaxes many of the rules and restrictions of formal written English. Generally, popular diction is the language of mass-media publications. Its aim is to appeal to and communicate clearly with the average reader.

27B Colloquialisms

This list contains some common misspellings, provincialisms, illiterate expressions, and incorrect forms to be avoided.

Not	But
aggravate	annoy, exasperate
a half an hour	a half hour or half an hour
alot	a lot
alright	all right
and etc.	etc. or et cetera
anywheres	anywhere
being that, being as how	as, because, since
can't seem to	seem unable to
considerable sick	quite sick
dark-complected	dark-complexioned
different than	different from
hadn't ought	ought not
heighth	height
irregardless	regardless, irrespective
no-account; no-good	worthless
off of	off, from
out loud	aloud
outside of	except; beside
should of, would of	should have, would have
the reason is because	the reason is that
tote	carry
try and give	try to give
use to	used to
visit with	visit
won him	beat him

Some colloquialisms and short forms are appropriate in everyday conversation and informal writing, but should not be used in formal written English.

Not	But
ad	advertisement
at about; at around	about; around
can't help but	cannot help but
center around	center on
get going	go
guess so, reckon so	think, suppose
has got to go	has to go
he is liable to be there	he is likely to be there
hold on	wait
kids	children
kind of a, sort of a	kind of, sort of
mighty hard	very hard
okay	all right
packs quite a punch	delivers a strong blow
phone	telephone
show up	appear to be superior
TV	television
wait a bit	wait

27C Here is a list of frequently misused or confused words; be sure you can distinguish their meanings

accept: to receive; to agree to (I *accept* your apology.)

except: to exclude (*Excepting* conscientious objectors is the job of the draft board only.)

except: a preposition meaning but, other than (*Except* for me, everyone caught a fish.)

affect: to influence (I was much *affected* by my father's musical preferences and talent.)

effect: to bring about (The heavy rains *effected* the end of the drought in California.)

effect: a noun meaning result (The *effect* of second-hand smoke is often lethal.)

allusion: indirect reference (Even an *allusion* to his nose can enrage him.)

illusion: false perception or image (The face he saw in the window was only an *illusion*.)

all ready: prepared (We were *all ready* for the hike to the top of Mt. Whitney.)

already: by this time (The rising tide had *already* flooded the homes on the beach.)

alumna: a female graduate (She was an *alumna* of Swarthmore.)

alumnae: two or more female graduates (Judy and Mary were *alumnae* of UCLA.)

alumnus: a male graduate (George was an *alumnus* of Columbia University.)

alumni: two or more male graduates; (In fact, George and his brother were *alumni*.); a universal term for college graduate (Most professionals in Ithaca are Cornell *alumni*.)

amount: used for non-countable bulk or weight (He drank only a small *amount* of milk.)

number: used for things that can be counted as individual units (Alta Dena Dairy produces a *number* of dairy products.)

compare: to deal with similarities

contrast: to deal with differences

complement: to complete or strengthen (The theater *complements* the mall by giving patrons a place to go either after shopping or after a movie.)

compliment: to praise (I felt I *complimented* him by buying four of his paintings.)

continual: frequently repeated (There are *continual* rains in Mexico City.)

continuous: without interruption; never ending (The *continuous* roar from Niagara Falls made conversation impossible.)

emigrate: to move out of a country or region (Many will *emigrate* to avoid the new tax laws.)

immigrate: to move into a country or region (The Pilgrims *immigrated* to the New World.)

fiancé: engaged man (plural: fiancés) (Phil is my *fiancé*. I have had two other fiancés.)

fiancee: engaged woman (plural: fiancees) (Mary is Jim's *fiancee*.)

former: first (If I had to choose between looks and money, I would choose the *former*.)

latter: last (If I had to choose between intelligence and talent, I would choose the *latter*.)

healthful: giving health (It is *healthful* to restrict your fat intake to 10% of your calories.)

healthy: having good health (My son is *healthy*; he is strong, energetic, and alert.)

imply: to suggest or hint by word or manner (He *implied*, by the way he ignored me, that he did not want to talk to me.)

infer: to gain an opinion or understanding from what one reads or hears (I *inferred* from the mayor's announcement that he was going to run.)

incredible: unbelievable (the story is *incredible*.)

incredulous: unwilling or unable to believe (the person is *incredulous*.)

less: used with non-countable items (We had *less* information about the war than they did.)

fewer: used with countable items (There were *fewer* students every year.)

principal: main, most important; a sum of money; a school official (Exeter's *principal* is John Phipps.)

principle: a rule of conduct; a general truth (A *principle* I never violate is to treat others with dignity.)

than: a conjunction used to express a comparison (She is more frugal *than* I am.)

then: at that time; therefore (He asked to marry her *then,* before he had met her parents.)

28 IMAGERY AND FIGURATIVE LANGUAGE

Writers in search of clear, vivid, and forceful prose often use devices called figures of speech to gain a desired effect. Note the image conveyed by Philip Wylie's description of a very thin woman as "a trellis for varicose veins." Among the important figures of speech are *simile, metaphor, synecdoche, metonymy,* and *personification.*

28A Simile

A simile is a figure of speech that uses *like* or *as* to compare two dissimilar things.

EXAMPLES:

". . .mountains like thirsty giants"—*National Geographic*

"a complexion like the belly of a fish"—*Charles Dickens*

Some similes have been used so much that they are no longer effective and are considered clichés.

INEFFECTIVE SIMILES:

old as the hills

dull as dishwater

American as apple pie

teeth like pearls

28B Metaphor

A metaphor is a figure of speech that suggests a likeness between two ideas or objects. *As* or *like* is not used.

EXAMPLES:

This monstrous human error, the megalopolis . . .

"She is the rose, the glory of the day."—*Edmund Spenser*

As with similes, some metaphors have become trite through overuse.

INEFFECTIVE METAPHORS:

the black sheep of the family

a wolf in sheep's clothing

a sea of troubles

A mixed metaphor results when metaphors occurring in the same sentence or paragraph create ludicrous images. If a woman is said to be a rose, and her arms petals, then she cannot be a jewel in the next sentence.

EXAMPLES:

The floodgates of atheism and permissiveness are stalking arm in arm throughout the land. (Floodgates cannot stalk.)

The harvest sown by the crooked politicians came home to roost. (Two mixed metaphors here: *seeds,* not a *harvest,* are sown, and *chickens,* not a *harvest,* come home to roost.)

28C Synecdoche

Synecdoche uses the part to represent the whole: *ranch hands,* for example, for a group of men performing labor with their hands, or *daily bread* for food. Here are a few more synecdoches:

The pen [writing] is mightier than the sword [fighting].

Five hundred souls [people] were lost.

28D Metonymy

Metonymy substitutes something closely related for the thing actually meant, for example: the *White House* stands for the president, *the Blue and the Gray,* for the Union and Confederate forces.

EXAMPLES:

"Scepter and crown [the king] must tumble down."

The Dodgers need to add more bats [good hitters] to their team.

I'm going to complain directly to City Hall.

28E Personification

Personification is a form of metaphor in which an inanimate object or abstract idea—for example, a car, or a quality like love—is treated as if it has human characteristics, feelings, or actions.

EXAMPLES:

"I have seen the ambitious ocean swell and rage and foam."

William Shakespeare

Justice hung her head.

We use personification often in daily conversation when we speak of the "bitter wind," "nasty weather," "gentle breeze," "cruel sea," "unforgiving clock," or "bountiful Mother Nature."

Errors involving these figures of speech often consist of mixed or confused examples, so be alert for any absurd, illogical, or meaningless expressions or comparisons.

28F Terms used in the discussion or analysis of poetry

Alexandrine, a verse line with six iambic feet (iambic hexameter)

Alliteration, the repetition of an initial letter or sound in two or more closely associated words or syllables:

"The fair breeze blew, the white foam flew,

The furrows followed free;"—Samuel Taylor Coleridge

Anacrusis, one or more extra unstressed syllables at the beginning of a line that are not a part of the regular meter of the poem

Anapest, a three-syllable foot with the third beat stressed (~ ~ +)

Assonance, repetition, or near repetition, of vowel sounds in two or more syllables: "I **s**aw old **Au**tumn in the misty morn"—Thomas Hood

Blank verse, poetry written in unrhymed iambic pentameter

Caesura, a pause in a line of poetry indicated by a comma, period, or other mark of punctuation

Catalexis, or **Truncation,** omission of the last, anticipated beat in a line of regular poetry

Consonance, repetition of the same consonant in close proximity:

"The curfew tolls the knell of parting day,"
—Thomas Gray

Couplet, a pair of rhymed lines of verse that make a complete statement:

Think what you will, we seize into our hand
His plate, his goods, his money, and his lands.
—William Shakespeare, *Richard II*

A heroic couplet is in iambic pentameter.

Dactyl, a three-syllable foot with the first beat stressed (+ ~ ~)

Dimeter, a poetic line of two feet

Double rhyme, a line with two rhyming syllables:

*The ship was **cheered,** the harbor **cleared**,"*
—Samuel Taylor Coleridge

Elision, the gradation of two syllables into one, as **ever** into **e're** or **over** into **o'er**

Foot, a measure or unit of rhythm comprising a definite, repeated pattern of stressed and unstressed syllables (See **iamb, trochee, anapest,** and **dactyl.**)

Free verse, poetry without regular meter or rhyme

Haiku, Japanese verse form of 17 syllables written according to strict rules

Heptameter, a poetic line of seven feet

Hexameter, a poetic line of six feet

Iamb, a two-syllable foot with the last beat stressed (~ +)

Iambic pentameter, a poetic line comprised of five iambic syllables

Limerick, a humorous verse that follows a strict pattern:

Five anapestic lines, the first, second, and fifth of which have three feet and rhyme; and the third and fourth of which have two feet and rhyme.

There was a young lady of Niger
Who smiled as she rode on a Tiger;
They came back from the ride
With the lady inside,
And the smile on the face of the Tiger.
—Anonymous

Meter, a beat established in a poem by the repetition of a predominant foot

Monometer, a poetic line of one foot

Octameter, a poetic line of eight feet

Octave, an eight-line stanza

Onomatopoeia, the use of words which convey their meaning in their pronunciation: *buzz, crackle, pop, sizzle*

Pathetic fallacy, the overuse of personification

Pentameter, a poetic line of five feet

Pyrrhic, a foot consisting of two unaccented syllables (~ ~).

Quatrain, a four-line stanza

Rhyme scheme, the arrangement of end rhymes in a poem

Rondel, a French verse form consisting of 13 or 14 lines and normally maintaining the rhyme scheme *ab*baab*ab*abba*ab*. The bold-face lines indicate pairs used as a refrain and wholly repeated.

Sestet, a six-line stanza

Sonnet, a fourteen-line poem written in the Italian or the Shakespearean form. The Italian form is made of an octave and a sestet, usually with the rhyme scheme **abbaabba cdecde.** The Shakespearean form has three quatrains and a couplet, with the rhyme scheme **abab cdcd efef gg.**

Sonnet sequence, a series of sonnets dealing with one theme

Spondee, a foot consisting of two accented syllables (+ +)

Stanza, a repeated division of a poem, usually with its own meter and rhyme scheme. A **stave** is a stanza intended to be sung.

Tanka, a Japanese poem of 31 syllables which deals with friendship, love, and nature

Tercet, or **triplet,** a three-line stanza or poem

Tetrameter, a poetic line of four feet

Trimeter, a poetic line of three feet

Triolet, a French verse form consisting of 8 lines and characterized by the repetition of whole lines. The rhyme scheme is *ab*aa*ab*ab. (The italicized letters indicate repetition of the entire line.)

Trochee, a two-syllable foot with the first beat stressed (+ ~)

Villanelle, a complex 19-line French poem divided into five tercets and a final four-line stanza. The rhyme scheme is *ab*A ab*a* ab*A* ab*a* ab*A* ab*a*A (The italicized letters indicate repetition of the entire line.)

29 WORDINESS

To avoid wordiness, eliminate language that either duplicates what has already been expressed or adds nothing to the sense of the statement.

WORDY:

At the present time, you can call up the library on the telephone if you want to receive that particular information.

REVISED:

Now you can call the library for that information.

WORDY:

A factor in the cause of the decline in stock prices was unwarranted growth.

REVISED:

One cause of the decline in stock prices was unwarranted growth.

OR

A factor in the decline in stock prices. . .

WORDY:

As a pet, the llama is easygoing in its habits and has a friendly personality.

REVISED:

As a pet, the llama is easygoing and friendly.

Expressions like *there are* and *it is* can add unnecessary words to your sentences.

EXAMPLES:

[There are] several people at school [who] have promised to help with the gardening at the new campus.

[It is] the way you swing the club [that] amazes me.

30 REDUNDANCY

A *redundant* expression is characterized by unnecessary repetition. To say *adequate enough* is to be redundant, because *adequate* and *enough* have nearly the same meaning.

EXAMPLES:

The two clubs joined [together] to feed the poor at Christmas.

They circled [around] the field.

For a list of ski areas in the state, refer [back] to page 25.

Avoid redundancies and roundabout phrases (*circumlocutions*) like the following:

Wordy	Concise
advance planning	planning
contributing factor	factor
due to the fact that	because
during the course of	during

Wordy	Concise
exact same symptoms	same symptoms; exact symptoms
for the purpose of	for
in the event that	if
in the near future	soon
large in size	large
past experience	experience
past history	history
revert back	revert
sufficient enough	sufficient; enough

31 OMISSIONS

A common error in written English is the careless omission, especially the omission acceptable in speech but not in writing. Some writers for whom English is a second language leave out the articles *a*, *an*, and *the* because their native languages uses them differently.

31A Careless omissions

Do not omit a needed verb, preposition, or conjunction.

FAULTY:

The Coast Guard always has and always will assist boaters in distress.

CORRECT:

The Coast Guard always has *assisted* and always will assist boaters in distress.

FAULTY:

Carol will graduate high school in June.

CORRECT:

Carol will graduate *from* high school in June.

FAULTY:

Liza was both allergic and fond of cats.

CORRECT:

Liza was both allergic *to* and fond of cats.

FAULTY:

He eats as much or more than anyone else in the family.

CORRECT:

He eats as much *as* or more than anyone else in the family.

31B Incomplete comparisons

Include every word needed to make a complete comparison.

INCOMPLETE:

Our new lawn requires less water.

REVISED:

Our new lawn requires less water *than our old one did.*

INCOMPLETE:

A subcompact's mileage is better than a large sedan.

REVISED:

A subcompact's mileage is better than *that of* a large sedan.

INCOMPLETE:

He wanted that medal more than his competitors. (Did he want the medal or the competitors?)

REVISED:

He wanted that medal more than his competitors *did* [want].

31C Missing transitions

Without logical transitions, the flow of ideas can lack natural progression and unity. Note the following:

WITHOUT TRANSITION:

He wanted so much to do well on the test; he had not studied enough.

REVISED:

He wanted so much to do well on the test, *but* he had not studied enough.

WITHOUT TRANSITION:

The multimillionaire Getty lived in London; most of his holdings were in the United States.

REVISED:

The multimillionaire Getty lived in London, *although* most of his holdings were in the United States.

32 SEXIST LANGUAGE

Throughout most of the history of the English language masculine pronouns have been used to represent either sex. In addition, women have been routinely excluded from many nouns intended to represent humanity. Still worse, traditional use of sexist language tends to place men and women in stereotyped roles.

It is not necessary to begin using awkward terms to avoid sexist language. Terms like *mail carrier, firefighter,* or *police officer* are reasonable alternatives to *mailman, fireman,* and *policeman.*

The use of the sexist pronoun is more difficult to avoid. One alternative is to use the plural: instead of *A voter must do his duty,* say *Voters must do their duty.* An occasional use of *he or she* is acceptable, though the phrase tends to be cumbersome.

EXAMPLE:

When a person is called by the IRS for an audit, *he or she* should go over last year's return.

You can avoid the construction by rewording the sentence.

EXAMPLE:

A person called by the IRS for an audit should go over the past year's return.

33 TWELVE MISTAKES THAT FAIL TESTS

(Arranged in order of Seriousness)

In my years of grading student writing, as well as in all the conversations I have had with colleagues about such grading, I have never quite understood the recurring and predictable state of approximately 20% of the papers turned in. These papers all fall below minimum standards, but they do so without a fight. By that, I mean that their authors commit errors and mental lapses that clearly they are capable of avoiding. Their writing is clear and direct, and their ideas are focused and right on target, but then they commit, in the lingo of chess players, a gross error. It's as if they did not care. Of course, I know they do care, but they experience these major lapses perhaps because they are stressed, depressed, anxious, or unsure of themselves. Here are the mistakes that comprise such gross errors, arranged, in my opinion, according to the magnitude of the damage they do to a paper's grade.

* *

1. NOTHING TO SAY

These papers are short, and often very neat. The student seems to have drawn a blank, and can think of nothing more to say than a well-phrased recapitulation of the question itself. This student obviously froze and would have done much better if he or she had thought a little *ahead of time* about how to develop an idea and maybe practiced on-the-spot writing. Assume a state of mental readiness for the act of writing.

Finding a Topic to Write On

After reading the essay question and prompts, most of the time you still have the job of choosing a topic. You will then have to organize the topic, supply adequate details, and write a direct and intelligent statement. If you cannot think of a truly exciting or innovative thesis for your paper, settle for something more mundane and manageable.

Above all, take a firm stand as you plan your essay. Your readers want to hear a controlling "voice" in your paper. Put your thesis statement in your first paragraph, and hide nothing. Your beginning should tell the reader what to expect and where this essay will be going. Look at the following beginning paragraph:

> I realized when I was assigned a post in Yarmouth, Maine that I would miss New York City. Little did I realize, however, that I would be so fundamentally affected by my move. Fortunately, I emerged from the whole experience much better off than when I started.

Notice that your whole essay is planned in this short beginning paragraph and now only requires detailed and careful development.

2. ALMOST BUT NOT QUITE

The student writes well, with attention to detail and supporting material. Unfortunately, though, this student does not read the question carefully and leaves out one of its main components. For example, once I administered a test with the following topic:

> Discuss a specific success or failure that taught you something important. Do not merely tell a story, but explain in detail how your experience affected your later attitudes and actions.

One of the best writers in the group composed an excellent essay about her experiences as a peace corps volunteer, concentrating on the success she had enjoyed helping the rural farmers in Salvador build a corn silo. Unfortunately, she did not complete Part II of the question, namely explaining how that experience affected her later attitudes and actions. She explained to me later that she felt she had really "creamed" the question, and had clearly demonstrated writing proficiency. I reminded her that she had missed perhaps 30% of the question, and had possibly demonstrated a carelessness in reading.

Always read the question more than once. Make a point to answer all parts. Reread the question *as you write*.

3. WITHOUT PERCEPTIBLE DIRECTION OR PURPOSE

That may be a little harsh, but the phrase "without direction or purpose" does come to mind when a grader is reading a paper that is without unity or coherence, that is, a paper that lacks proper arrangement or sequence of ideas. The ideas are usually there, but they are so misplaced that they are not available to the reader on a first perusal of the paper. Usually the questions students are given on extemporaneous essay questions, for example, are clearly posed and direct. They have to be, because the test must be understood by a vast number of very different constituents, some of whom employ English as a second language. As Henry James said to his brother, "For God's sake, William, just say it!" Have a good general point to every paragraph, and then support that general point with cogent and direct data. Think, *ahead of time,* about the qualities of *unity* and *coherence* in written work. Be sure the concepts are clear in your mind; do not neglect them when you write your essay.

A. Lack of Unity

Every point you bring up in an essay needs to contribute to a SINGLE idea or thesis. A paragraph is unified when each sentence contributes to developing a central thought. Each single thought developed in each paragraph must contribute, in turn, to the single idea that unifies the essay.

If you are writing a paragraph in which you argue that fast food is nutritious, you must discuss *how* or *in what way* fast food is nutritious in virtually everything you say. You can say that fish and chips contains protein and niacin, you can say that potatoes contribute needed fiber, and you can say that pizza contains cheese rich in protein and calcium. You cannot discuss the fact that McDonald's outlets are more numerous than Jack-in-the-Box outlets, or the fact that your brother works at Carl's Jr. The key to avoiding papers that are disunified is to concentrate on a single point. Use the *pregnant sentence* method of development discussed in section 24B. If you need to add more to what you have written, add it by *becoming more detailed, concrete, and specific about what you have already said* rather than by adding new and disparate thoughts.

Suppose, in other words, that you are writing an essay about the fact that classes fill too quickly during registration and you find yourself without a great deal to say. Try explaining more and more *minute* portions of the problem; go *into* your subject more and more. Put on microscopic glasses and dive into the inner world of your main idea. Describe how students camp on the doorstep of the registrar's office at five in the morning in order to have a chance to sign up for a class they need, or that more and more instructors are being lobbied for add-ons even during the previous semester, or that many students spend five years in college because they cannot sign up for the classes they need, or that some students have to drive to three different schools to have a full schedule, or that students on various types of aid must have twelve units, or that some infrequently offered requirements fill up so quickly that it is conceivable that some majors may never finish college. Observations such as these are the fine details that make a point dramatic and important because they all converge in the pregnant sentence that lies at the heart of your statement.

B. Lack of Coherence

Coherence is the quality of sticking together, that is, of *ideas* sticking together in a composition. One sentence should lead naturally to the next, and each new idea should evolve from a previous one. Without a logical progression of ideas, an essay becomes *incoherent,* a word which has become synonymous with *not understandable*. A writer achieves coherence by being careful how he or she arranges a string of ideas. They have to be in a sensible order. If you are discussing events or actions, they must be in **chronological order.** If you are explaining the negative effect of a recession on universities, let us say, you might choose **order of importance** as your arrangement scheme. Often the movement within a composition or paragraph is from **general to specific.** If you are describing something, usually you describe it in **spatial order.** There are many other arrangement plans, **problem-solution, question-answer, topic-illustration.** None are difficult to use; the trick is to be sure to use a plan consistently that is clear to the writer, and that is appropriate for the topic being developed. Make sure you know what you want to say and what sequence you want to follow. Take the trouble to phrase each sentence so that it flows grammatically and logically from what you have written before.

Acquire the art of using transitional devices, which are essential in achieving coherence. Some of the important ones are the use of pronouns, the repetition of key words or ideas, the use of conjunctions and other transitional expressions like the following:

To signal *additions:*

> also, and, besides, equally important, first, second, third (etc.), further, furthermore, in addition, too, next

To signal *similarities:*

> likewise, in the same manner, each in its turn, similarly

To signal *differences:*

> but, in contrast, however, on the other hand, on the contrary

To signal *examples* or *intensity:*

> after all, even, for example, for instance, indeed, in fact, it is true, specifically, that is, to illustrate, truly

To signal *place:*

> above, adjacent to, below, elsewhere, nearby, on the other side, opposite to, to the left

To signal *time:*

> after a while, before, during, earlier, finally, first, immediately, later, simultaneously, when, then, while, subsequently, as long as, at length, at that time, at last

4. MAJOR SENTENCE ERRORS

It is safe to say that students are almost always expected to write complete sentences and that there are no gray areas where run-on or fragmented sentences are acceptable. If you have a tendency to make sentence errors in your writing, that is, **fragments, comma splices,** or **fused sentences,** you need to take steps to rid your writing of such errors **before** you submit a paper. If you are not sure if you make such errors, visit your campus tutorial or writing lab and ask if someone there will evaluate your writing. Most tutorial centers and writing clinics have a number of computer-aided instructional programs that do wonders for students who are not clear in their minds what a sentence really is. Do not attempt to avoid sentence errors by writing primer-style sentences. Essays that begin, "I believe a good education is important. I believe men and women should have it. A good education is what makes a good life" will, at least, be graded down as lower-than-college-level writing. Take the time to rid your writing of fundamental sentence errors before you turn in papers.

* *

The lone or infrequent occurrence of the errors that are discussed from here on is no longer in the "gross" category and is less damaging to a student's score than the faults described up to this point. However, you can be sure that the errors will be noticed, and, if they or combinations of them occur with frequency, they will cause a student to lose credit and possibly even fail a writing assignment.

* *

"Bermuda Triangle Errors"

I have found that many students have their own custom Bermuda Triangle when it comes to writing, their own set of grammatical or writing problems that never ceases to make them nervous when they enter those waters. Jim, for example, never quite knew how to use cases. He seemed to believe that the use of the pronoun **me** was always wrong, so wrong, that whenever he said or wrote it, he would sound really bad. He would write, "The coach gave Phil Lozano and *I* three days to straighten out." (Just to keep the record straight, he should have written the objective form of the pronoun, *me*, because it is receiving action). Another student of mine, Ed, always became befuddled when he used gerund phrases with a possessive pronoun. He would say, "*Me* staying out late with my buddies is all right with my girlfriend." (He should have written "*My* staying out late is all right with my girlfriend.") Many of my students say that some teacher in their past strongly warned them not to write in the first person, "*I*." (The truth is there is nothing wrong with using the first person as your point-of-view; in fact, most questions asked on a timed writing test deal with personal reminiscence and experience and require a first-person response.) What most students remember having been told about the pronoun *I* is that it should not be used in severely *formal, elevated* discourse, and it should not be mixed with an already-establish third-person point of view (*he, she,* or *it*).

If, like many students, you feel nervous when you write, perhaps it is because you have a few areas in writing that bother you, and you write perfectly well otherwise. For example, do you have problems with the use of the nominative and objective case? Are you frequently unsure of *who-whom*, or *I-me* options? My advice to you is that you think a bit about your rough areas (we all have them), trap or isolate them, and then complete the relatively minor job of studying and memorizing that will rid yourself of the problem for good. If you need further help identifying your errors, there are many good diagnostic English surveys. Check with your English teacher, counselor, or tutoring lab.

5. ERRORS IN PREDICATION OR MIXED SENTENCES

Predication refers to the process of joining the *naming* part of the sentence (the *subject*) to the *doing* or *describing* part of a sentence (the *predicate*). Mixed sentences occur when the writer equates unlike constructions or ideas. Look at the following incorrect examples.

MIXED:

> By working at such technical plants as Lockheed and Bendix gives the engineering students insight into what will be expected of them. (*By working* does not give them insight; *working* does.)

CORRECTED:

> Working at such technical plants as Lockheed and Bendix gives the engineering students insight into what will be expected of them.

MIXED:

> Among those who take the writing examination, they do not all have to take it again. (The modifying phrase beginning with *Among* requires

a noun that gives an amount, such as *sixty percent* or *many*, not the general *they*.)

CORRECTED:

More than three-quarters of those who take the writing examination do not have to take it again.

MIXED:

A writing proficiency examination is when you write an essay right on the spot. (Written definitions require nouns or noun clauses on both sides of *be*).

CORRECTED:

A writing proficiency examination is writing an essay on the spot.

MIXED:

The reason I decided to buy an American car is because I felt sorry for American auto workers. (The words *reason* and *because* both imply the same thing, namely *purpose*.)

CORRECTED:

The reason I decided to buy an American car is that I felt sorry for American auto workers.

Be sure that all parts of your sentences, particularly the subjects and predicates, fit together grammatically and logically.

6. SUBJECT-VERB AGREEMENT ERRORS

Nouns, verbs, and pronouns often have endings or special forms that signal number, that is, whether or not the word is singular or plural; it is a principle that a verb always agrees in number with its subject.

SINGULAR:

The *cat* in the alley *looks* hungry.

PLURAL:

The *cats* in the alley *look* hungry.

Make sure a pronoun agrees in number with the noun it is taking the place of, its antecedent.

SINGULAR:

A teenage *girl* has *her* own language.

PLURAL:

Teenage *girls* have *their* own language.

Sentences that are uncomplicated, such as those above, do not present problems for most writers. It is in sentences where words or groups of words come between the subject and verb that students are tripped up. Here are some guidelines to help you avoid the problem:

• Be sure of the number of the subject. Sometimes it is not so easy a matter to decide. Collective nouns such as *class, herd, audience, half, part, crowd,* and *most* can be either singular or plural, since they can refer either to a collective unit or to separate entities. Take the following examples (all correct):

-Half of the class are failing.

-Half of the class is devoted to the study of torts.

-Part of the herd are suffering from heat exhaustion.

-Part of the herd is going to be sold to the Triangle Ranch.

-Half of the crowd are buying popcorn, souvenirs, and the like.

-Half of the crowd is doing the wave.

• Be sure the verb agrees with the subject, even though the normal word order is inverted, as in questions or expletive constructions (*there is* or *there are*). Here are some examples (all correct):

- Is the AIDS virus harmless or contagious?

- Are Beatrice and Ed really married?

- Is the citizens versus the City of San Jose trial over yet?

- There are, after the appeal has been heard, two directions we can take.

- After many arguments and separations, there is reconcilement in the air.

• Be sure subjects and verbs agree, even when other words come between them. Here are examples (all correct):

- A slew of new IRS regulations and restrictions bewilders taxpayers every year.

- The violations made by the Meat Packing Union are staggering in number.

- One of my sons is a soldier.

7. DANGLING OR MISPLACED MODIFIER

The arrangement of words in sentences usually tells the reader how the words are related. Sometimes, however, a sentence is confused if the reader cannot connect modifiers to the words they describe. To avoid confusion or ambiguity, place the modifying words, phrases, or clauses near the words they modify.

CONFUSING:

The electric pencil sharpener needs repair in the mail room.

CORRECT:

The electric pencil sharpener *in the mail room* needs repair.

CONFUSING:

He packed all of the books and fine photographs into his van, which he was donating to the library.

CORRECT:

He packed all of the books and fine photographs *which he was donating to the library* into his van.

CONFUSING:

In designing the new science building, a venting system was overlooked.

CORRECT:

> In designing the new science building, *the architects overlooked* the venting system.

8. MISUSE OR OVERUSE OF SEMICOLON

The semicolon can be used as a "weak period" to separate closely related sentences. It cannot be used to separate a subordinate clause or a phrase from the main sentence.

WRONG:

> According to the Labor Bureau; more women are working today than ever.

REVISED:

> According to the Labor Bureau, more women are working today than ever.

The semicolon cannot be used to introduce a series.

WRONG:

> Most instructors have heard the standard reasons for not finishing a paper on time; a death in the family, illness, a sudden rush at the workplace.

REVISED:

> Most instructors have heard the standard reasons for not finishing a paper on time: a death in the family, illness, a sudden rush at the workplace.

Overuse of the semicolon leads to over-coordinated sentences and ideas. Use the semicolon only to join coordinated elements. Avoid using it too often; instead, use the principles of subordination.

9. PROBLEMS WITH VERB TENSE

The choice of the appropriate tense usually presents few problems in papers of students who are native speakers of English. Those problems that do occur usually involve the use of the present tense in a special sense or uses of the perfect tenses.

The present tense generally signifies action at the time the subject is speaking, as in *Fritz knows the answer* or *I am making your eggs right this moment*. It is also used in a few special cases.

To indicate recurring or habitual action

> The college police generally *use* common sense.

> The train in Switzerland always *runs* on time.

To state a universal or timeless or general truth

> The sun *is* the source of all energy.

> The early bird *gets* the worm.

To discuss or recapitulate action occurring in literature, plays, film

> In *Wuthering Heights*, Heathcliff really *loves* Catherine Earnshaw.

> In the *Old Testament*, Abraham *prepares* to sacrifice his only begotten son, Isaac.

To indicate future time

> Remember that Spring Break *comes* early this year.

The perfect tenses all use the helping verb *have* in their formation in conjunction with the past participle of the verb. It is in the identification of the past participle that students slip. Here are the principal parts of some particularly troublesome verbs in this regard:

Infinitive	Present Tense	Past Tense	Past Participle
to arise	arise	arose	arisen
to bid	bid	bid	bid
to choose	choose	chose	chosen
to speak	speak	spoke	spoken
to sink	sink	sank	sunk
to drive	drive	drove	driven
to ride	ride	rode	ridden
to hang (suspend)	hang	hung	hung
to hang (execute)	hang	hanged	hanged
to tear	tear	tore	torn
to wear	wear	wore	worn
to shake	shake	shook	shaken
to stand	stand	stood	stood
to steal	steal	stole	stolen
to spring	spring	sprang	sprung
to swim	swim	swam	swum
to throw	throw	threw	thrown
to go	go	went	gone
to drink	drink	drank	drunk
to sit	sit	sat	sat
to set	set	set	set

If you have had trouble with verb forms in the past, practice the use of these forms, particularly in forming perfect tenses, because that process is where most students make verb errors.

A good way to practice is to spend some time forming perfect tenses for each of the verbs listed, using the models below:

PRESENT PERFECT TENSE

Person	Helping Verb	Past Participle
Singular		
I	have	_____
you	have	_____
he, she, it	has	_____
Plural		
we	have	_____
you	have	_____
they	have	_____

PAST PERFECT TENSE

Person	Helping Verb	Past Participle
Singular		
I	had	_____
you	had	_____
he, she, it	had	_____
Plural		
we	had	_____
you	had	_____
they	had	_____

FUTURE PERFECT TENSE

Person	Helping Verb	Past Participle
Singular		
I	shall have	_____
you	will have	_____
he, she, it	will have	_____
Plural		
we	shall have	_____
you	will have	_____
they	will have	_____

Take the time to use proper verb forms in all your writing.

10. THOUGHTLESS USE OF THE PASSIVE VOICE

Action verbs have two **voices**, the **active voice** and the **passive voice**. Through the use of voices, verbs that take objects (transitive verbs) can show whether their subjects are acting or acted upon. In the active voice, the subject *does* the action:

Harvey started the engine.

The professor coordinated the writing program.

Elizabeth earned a degree in health sciences.

In the **passive voice**, the subject *receives* the action:

The writing test is taken by 3500 students every year.

The engine is started many times a day.

The term paper was written by Norma Garza.

To form the passive voice, the writer employs the verb *to be* as a helping verb, adding it to the past participle of the main verb.

PASSIVE CONJUGATION OF THE VERB *TO GIVE*, 3RD-PERSON SINGULAR

	Helping Verb To Be	Past Participle of Main Verb
Present Tense:	he is	given
Past Tense:	he was	given
Future Tense:	he will be	given
Present Perfect Tense:	he has been	given
Past Perfect Tense:	he had been	given
Future Perfect Tense:	he will have been	given

To change a verb from the passive to the active voice, we convert the verb's subject into an object and replace it with a new one:

PASSIVE:

Phil *was given* a plaque by the senior class.

ACTIVE:

The senior class *gave* Phil a plaque.

PASSIVE:

The ruling about the deductibility of loan costs *was changed* by the IRS.

ACTIVE:

The IRS *changed* the ruling about the deductibility of loan costs.

Notice how the passive voice sentences seem to lack punch, and how they are wordier than the active versions. Because the passive leaves out or de-emphasizes the actor (the performer of the verb's action), it is often ambiguous or confusing.

WEAK PASSIVE:

The writing test was felt by the students to be difficult because they were not given adequate time to rewrite and proofread their work.

STRONG ACTIVE:

The students thought the writing test difficult because it gave them inadequate time to rewrite and proofread their work.

The passive voice is appropriate in two contexts: when the receiver of the action is more important than the doer, and when the doer is unknown.

The vice-president *was murdered* this afternoon.

(The murderer is presumably unknown, and the vice-president's death is the important point.)

On the first trial, ethyl alcohol was added to the gasoline.

(The person who added the alcohol is incidental to the fact that it was added. The passive voice is used frequently in scientific writing.)

Prefer the active voice to the passive voice, except when the doer of the action is unknown or unimportant.

11. INEFFECTIVE COORDINATION AND SUBORDINATION

Establishing understandable and coherent relationships between ideas is the main function of subordination and coordination.

To *subordinate* is to "move to a lower structural rank." The italicized passages in the following sentence are subordinated.

When the oxygen gas in the bloodstream drops to the .06 level, the surgeon must decide whether or not to go in again, *the risks of open-heart surgery vying in his mind with the risks of heart failure.*

Although the ideas carried in the grammatically subordinate structures are very important, subordinating them emphasizes the main clause and establishes their relationship to the ideas carried in the main clause. The sentence has one point, and that one point is given weight and importance by the subordinated ideas. One of the marks of a seasoned writer is the ability to subordinate skillfully.

To *coordinate* is to "make equal in structural rank." The italicized passages in the following sentence are coordinated.

The precious oil we burn is finite, but *trees and their derivatives alcohol and methane are self-renewing.*

WAYS TO COORDINATE AND SUBORDINATE IDEAS IN THE SENTENCE

Use **coordination** to link ideas of equal weight

1. Join main clauses with a comma and a coordinating conjunction (*and, but, for, or, yet, so*).

   The Gulf War liberated Kuwait, *and* it lifted the hearts of millions of Americans.

2. Join main clauses with a semicolon alone or a semicolon used with a conjunctive adverb: *although, nevertheless, therefore, however, consequently*, etc.

   He was very aware of the dangers of smoking; *nevertheless* he continued to smoke two packs a day.

3. Within clauses, connect words and phrases with coordinating conjunctions: *and, but, or, nor*.

   The trombones *and* trumpets became louder, and the whole crescendo of the orchestra *and* chorus shook the building.

Use **subordination** to position ideas logically and unambiguously

1. Subordinate a clause by beginning it with a subordinating conjunction: *if, unless, before, after, since, when, because, as, how, if*, etc.

   Before inflation consumes our collective savings and our retirement systems, we must lower the national debt.

2. Use relative pronouns (*who, that, which, what*) to subordinate clauses that are more logically adjective or noun clauses.

   The leader *who attracted the most attention last year* was Saddam Hussein.

3. Use a phrase to carry a subordinate idea.

   Between the compressor and the fan lies the master cylinder. (prepositional phrase)

   The window *broken by the fury of the hurricane* allowed enough water in *to destroy the contents of the room.* (participial phrase; infinitive phrase)

   My son, *a soldier with the 3rd Armored Division,* spent several weeks in Iraq. (appositive phrase).

4. Use a simple modifier.

   The reason *sprawling* Los Angeles is *not attractive* as a city is that *greedy* builders put up *relatively cheap* and *architecturally incompatible* structures.

Use coordination to link equal words and ideas. Use subordination to de-emphasize ideas less important than the main idea.

12. ERRORS IN PARALLELISM

Whenever we list two or more words in a series, we make sure they are grammatically identical:

George, Fred, and *Pete* went hunting on Monday.

I enjoy most nuts, but particularly *peanuts, walnuts,* and *chestnuts.*

Suppose they are not identical:

The campers ate a hearty meal of *tuna sandwiches, scrumptious,* and *swallowed.*

The sentence makes no sense because it is a principle in all writing that words and ideas of equal importance are constructed alike. Nouns are used with other nouns, verbs with other verbs of the same tense, adverbs with other adverbs, and so on. Parallelism is essential in writing because readers of English expect balance and symmetry in any coordinate sequence.

AWKWARD:

As a lecturer, he was rude, with intimidating gestures, and he calls some students names.

PARALLEL:

As a lecturer, he was rude, intimidating, and insulting.

AWKWARD:

His wife gave him a day runner with a calculator and even having a digital watch and a radio.

PARALLEL:

His wife gave him a day runner with a calculator, a digital watch, and even a radio.

Sometimes the parallel structure simply needs to be pointed up by the repetition of a strategic word or words.

AWKWARD:

The Reverend Taylor wanted the church elders to establish liaisons with local business organizations, offering the resources of the church to the chamber of commerce, and schedule arts and hobby classes that were desired by everyone.

PARALLEL:

The Reverend Taylor wanted the church elders to establish liaisons with local business organizations, *to* offer the resources of the church to the chamber of commerce, and *to* schedule arts and hobby classes that were desired by everyone.

AWKWARD:

The keynote speech was interminable, repetitious, and could not easily be heard.

PARALLEL:

The keynote speech was interminable, repetitious, and inaudible.

Errors in parallelism are often made after correlatives— *either–or, neither–nor, whether–or, both–and, not only–but also.*

AWKWARD:

Modern classical music is neither inspiring nor did I find it intellectually fulfilling. (An adjective made parallel with a clause.)

PARALLEL:

Modern classical music is neither inspiring nor fulfilling (Two parallel adjectives).

AWKWARD:

Not only are the gang members spraying graffiti all over the brick walls of the campus but also in adjacent residential neighborhoods. (A clause made parallel with a prepositional phrase.)

PARALLEL:

Not only are the gang members spraying graffiti all over the brick wall of the campus, but they are also spraying in adjacent neighborhoods. (Two parallel clauses.)

Maintain parallelism in sentences that have two or more equal ideas.

34 DOCUMENTATION

Students writing term papers for the first time should be aware that **documentation** is as important as the content of their paper. What is more, the *quality* of the documentation, of its form and exactness, usually signifies the general worth and credibility of the paper.

WHAT DO YOU DOCUMENT?

You document, that is, *reveal the source of,* any idea that you borrowed, any quotation, any facts, data, charts, or statistics, or narratives. In addition, you must acknowledge any *idea* that you borrow, any line of thought, or any original phrase or sentence.

WHY DO YOU DOCUMENT?

You document to avoid plagiarism, or representation of someone else's work as your own, an easy mistake to make when you are writing a term paper based on a large number of secondary sources. You document sources to let your reader know where you got your information and how current it is in the event that the reader wants to build on your thesis and carry it forward. For this reason, careful documentation can be considered the heart and soul of scholarship. Finally, you document your sources because you wish to make your work more convincing and substantial; this is the evidence that hammers home your point and renders your work authoritative.

34A BIBLIOGRAPHY

A bibliography is simply a list of books, journal articles, and other research materials related to a particular subject. Bibliographies can be either generalized or specific. For example, there are bibliographies that are collections of titles on wheat production, or collections of biographies, or collections of book titles on hunting, or collections of criticisms on Charles Dickens' novels, or even collections of critical articles about one of his novels, such as *Great Expectations*. The sources actually cited and listed alphabetically on a separate sheet at the end of the paper is called *References* in the APA (American Psychological Association) style of documentation, *Works Cited* in the MLA (Modern Language

Association) style, and *Bibliography* in CMS (*Chicago Manual of Style*) style. If you list all the books you have read as background, regardless of whether or not you have cited them within the text of your document, you may call the list *Bibliography* in the APA style or *Works Consulted* in the MLA style; the CMS allows *Sources Consulted, Works Cited,* or *Selected Bibliography,* if they better describe your list. The list of notes corresponding to the superscript numerals in the CMS method of documentation is called *Notes*.

34B MLA documentation

The style of documentation described in the *MLA Handbook for Writers of Research Papers** uses parenthetical citations in the written material to document all sources of quotations, paraphrased statements, ideas, or other secondary sources. These parenthetical citations refer to a list of *Works Cited,* a complete and detailed list of references at the end of the paper. Typically, the author's name is mentioned in a sentence that introduces the material, and a page number in parentheses is given at the end of the sentence. For more information about the source, all the reader has to do is find the author's name in the *Works Cited* page at the end of the essay. MLA style also permits the addition of a series of explanatory notes for explanation or interpretation. Superscript (or *raised*) numbers are used in the essay to refer readers to a list of notes that follows the end of the report under the heading of *NOTES*. For full information about the MLA style, consult the official MLA style manual in your library or bookstore.

EXAMPLES:

Of a citation in the text:

Howard Lear concludes that William Faulkner was very fond of the residents of Yoknapatawpha County, even though he frequently cast moral aspersions upon them (118).

Of an entry in the Works Cited list:

Osborne, David, and Ted Gaebler. Reinventing

Government: How the Entrepreneurial Spirit

Is Transforming the Public Sector. Reading:

Addison, 1992.

DOCUMENTING SOURCES WITHIN THE TEXT

MLA textual references can be made in three ways:

1. By citing the author's last name and the page numbers of the source in parentheses.

Some major critics argue that the emphasis on linguistics and the dynamics of language brought forward by the newest critical modes may spell a renaissance in modern poetry (Waller 28).

2. By referring to the author in the text and placing only the page numbers in parentheses.

*Gibaldi, Joseph. *MLA Handbook for Writers of Research Papers*. 4th ed. New York: MLA, 1995.

Carl Resener categorizes the homeless according to the reasons for their displacement: the "Seekers," the "Mentally Ill," the "Stranded," and the "Self-inflicted" (29-42).

3. By simply referring to the author in the text, omitting parenthetical reference.

Leggett condemns the entire scope of contemporary entertainment and amusement as incapable of provoking any educational or intellectual aftermath in the minds of the participating American public.

MECHANICS OF THE PARENTHETICAL REFERENCE

The great advantage of the MLA method of documentation is that it allows you to document a source briefly and clearly. There are three ways you can insert your references to sources in your text:

1. Place the author's last name and the page number(s) of the source in parentheses before the final period of the sentence containing the citation.

   "Berenice" is seemingly cut from the same psychological cloth as his acknowledged masterpieces, and the reader at once recognizes the familiar hallmarks of Poe's work, "a somber Gothic setting, remote and distant time and locale, a narrative woven of psychological aberrations which reflect upon and illuminate the human mind" (Burson 45).

2. For clarity, place the reference *within* the sentence to make clear its relationship to one part of your statement.

   While Burson concludes that the popular short story "is not a horror story at all, but rather a humorous and sometimes wildly comic commentary on the Gothic tale as Poe understood it" (48), there is no doubt that "Berenice" has always been considered a serious tale of horror.

3. If you are documenting a quotation of more than four lines set off from the text, place the reference at the end of the quotation two spaces *after* the final period. Follow the MLA recommendations for spacing displayed quotations of four or more lines from the body of your paper:

   • Double space before and after the quotation.

   • Indent ten spaces from the left margin.

   • Double-space the quoted lines.

   If the reader is misled by these passages, that is, if he believes that the author is in earnest, he may be relying too much on the lofty style of Poe's language: his elaborate periodic sentences, the almost oratorical rhythm of his lines, the layers of description or restatement that lend credence to his ideas, his use of classical names or allusions, his frequent employment of quotations in other languages, his dramatic expressions like *Alas!* or *Ah!*, his implied superiority over the reader in facile citations from sophisticated or occult spheres of knowledge, his minute distinctions of word or thought that pretend fine intellect. It is just this style that is being parodied, in fact, by the nonsensical nature of what is being so impressively described. (Burson 55)

MECHANICS OF THE "WORKS CITED" SECTION

The following examples provide models for frequently cited sources.

A Book by One Author

Wylie, Philip. Generation of Vipers. New York: Rinehart, 1942.

Two or More Books by One Author

Grisham, John. The Firm. New York: Bantam, 1991.
—. A Time to Kill. New York: Bantam, 1989.
—. The Pelican Brief. New York: Doubleday, 1992.

A Book by Two or Three Authors

Osborne, David, and Ted Gaebler. Reinventing Government: How the Entrepreneurial Spirit Is Transforming the Public Sector. Reading: Addison, 1992.

A Book by Four or More Authors

Ehrenhaft, George, et al. How to Prepare for the ACT. New York: Barron's, 1991.
OR
Ehrenhaft, George, Robert. L. Lehrman, Allan Mundsack, and Fred Obrecht. How to Prepare for the ACT. New York: Barron's, 1991.

A Book by an Anonymous Author

The Key to English: Figurative Expressions. 1968 ed. New York: Macmillan, 1968.

A Book with an Editor

Bucker, William E., ed. Prose of the Victorian Period. Boston: Houghton, 1958.

A Book with an Author and an Editor

Verne, Jules. Voyage from the Earth to the Moon.
    Ed. Anthony Boucher. New York: Dodd,
    1956.
OR, if you are citing the *editor's* work:
Boucher, Anthony, ed. Voyage from the Earth to the
    Moon. By Jules Verne. New York: Dodd,
    1956.

A Work in an Anthology

Huxley, Thomas Henry. "Science and Culture."
    Prose of the Victorian Period. Ed. William E.
    Buckler. Boston: Houghton, 1958. 24-33.

Several References to a Textbook, Casebook, or Anthology

First, make an initial reference to the anthology:

Jacobus, Lee, ed. A World of Ideas. Boston:
    Bedford Books, 1994.

Then, make cross-references to the initial reference:

Darwin, Charles. Natural selection. In Jacobus, pp.
    403-415.
Bacon, Francis. "The Four Idols." In Jacobus, pp.
    385-397.

A Work in Several Volumes

Johnson, Edgar. Charles Dickens: His Tragedy and
    Triumph. 2 vols. New York: Simon, 1952.

A Second or Later Edition

Azar, Betty Schrampfer. Understanding and Using
    English Grammar. 2nd ed. Englewood Cliffs:
    Prentice, 1989.

A Book in a Series

Piper, Henry Dan, ed. Fitzgerald's The Great
    Gatsby: The Novel, The Critics, The
    Background. Scribner Research Anthologies.
    New York: Scribners, 1970.

A Translation

Hsueh-chin, Tsao. Dream of the Red Chamber.
    Trans. Chi-Chen Wang. Garden City:
    Doubleday, 1958.

A Signed Article in a Reference Book

Wiley, Basil. "Arnold, Matthew." Encyclopedia
    Britannica. 1979 ed.

An Unsigned Article in a Reference Book

"Postal Union, Universal." The World Book
    Encyclopedia. 1989 ed.

An Article in a Journal with Continuous Pagination

Palmer, Glenn E. "Computer Applications in the
    Freshman Laboratory." Journal of Chemical
    Education 58 (1981): 995.

An Article in a Journal That Paginates Each Issue Separately

Cummins, Paul. "Teaching Modern Poetry."
    California English Journal 5.2 (1969): 43-46.

An Article from a Monthly Publication

Williamson, Marianne. "A Return to Love."
    Cosmopolitan Dec. 1992: 66-68.

An Article from a Weekly Publication

Nicklin, Julie L. "New Technologies Extend the
    Reach of Many College Fund Raisers." The
    Chronicle of Higher Education 25 Nov. 1992:
    A13-A14.

A Signed Article from a Daily Newspaper

Burns, John F. "Stranger in a Strange Land: Muslim
    in Serb Army." New York Times 7 Jan. 1993,
    sec. 1:A3.

An Unsigned Article from a Daily Newspaper

"Nationsbank Card Features a Savings Plan." New
    York Times 7 Jan. 1993, sec. C:5.

An Editorial

"The Clintons Go Private." Editorial. Daily News 6
    Jan. 1993: 10.

Lectures, Speeches, and Addresses

Clinton, Bill. Inaugural Address. Inauguration.
    Washington, D.C., 20 Jan. 1992.

A Book by a Corporate Author

The Invitation to Learning Reader. 7 vols. New
    York: CBS, 1953.

Interviews

Miller, Barbara. Telephone interview. 22 Oct.
    1992.
OR

Bradley, Thomas. Personal interview. 15 Jan.
    1992.

ELECTRONIC DOCUMENTS

Electronic media are of two main types: (1) CD-ROMS, disks, or tapes that you physically carry with you and load into your computers; (2) on-line resources such as information you find on the Internet, listserv mail, or e-mail. In both cases you can print out the resource and document it in the same way as printed material.

The same basic information is required (whatever is available to you):

-Author (if given)

-Title of the source

-Date you first consulted the source

-Publication media (CD-ROM; ON-LINE)

-Name of the computer service if there is one

-Identifying numbers or the pathway needed for retrieval of the material

-Date of access (or date the source was posted on-line)

Material on CD-ROM

"United States v. Shabani, document no. 93-981." U.S. Supreme Ct., reproduced in SIRS Government Reporter. CD-ROM. Boca Raton, FL: Social Issues Resources Series, 1995.

Material on Disk

McBride, Joyce. A Letter to My Mother. Disk. Worcester: Eastgate, 10 March 1997.

Material Accessed via Networks

King, John. "Sex, lies, and the Internet." Microsoft Internet Magazine, [magazine on-line] March 1998. 8 June 1998 <http://home.microsoft.com/reading/archives/feature-3-2-98.asp>

Pablos-Mendez, A., Raviglione, M.C., Laszlo, A., Binkin, N., Rieder, H.L., Bustreo, F., Cohn, D., Lambregts-van Weezenbeek, C.S., Kim, S.J., Chaulet, P., & Nunn, P. "Global Surveillance for Antituberculosis-Drug Resistance." New England Journal of Medicine. 4 June 1998. 12 June 1998 <http://www.nejm.org/public/1998/0338/0023/1641/1.html>

E-Mail and Other Electronic Messages

Patterson, E. Re: "Faulkner Summer Seminar." E-mail to Fred Obrecht accessed 8 June 1996.

MLA-STYLE SHORTENED PUBLISHERS' NAMES

SHORT FORM	PUBLISHER'S COMPLETE NAME
ALA	American Library Association
Allyn	Allyn and Bacon, Inc.
Appleton	Appleton-Century-Crofts
Ballantine	Ballantine Books, Inc.
Bantam	Bantam Books, Inc.
Barnes	Barnes and Noble Books
Barron's	Barron's Educational Series, Inc.
Basic	Basic Books
CAL	Center for Applied Linguistics
Cambridge UP	Cambridge University Press
Clarendon	Clarendon Press
Columbia UP	Columbia University Press
Dell	Dell Publishing Co., Inc.
Dodd	Dodd, Mead, and Co.
Doubleday	Doubleday and Co., Inc.
Eastgate	Eastgate Systems
ERIC	Educational Resources Information Systems
Farrar	Farrar, Straus and Giroux, Inc.
GPO	Government Printing Office
Harcourt	Harcourt Brace Jovanovich, Inc.
Harper	HarperCollins Publishers
Harvard UP	Harvard University Press
Heath	D. C. Heath and Co.
Holt	Holt, Rinehart and Winston, Inc.
Houghton	Houghton Mifflin Co.
Knopf	Alfred A. Knopf, Inc.
Lippincott	J. B. Lippincott Co.
Little	Little, Brown, and Company, Inc.
Macmillan	Macmillan Publishing Co., Inc.
McGraw	McGraw-Hill, Inc.
NEA	The National Education Association
Norton	W.W. Norton and Co., Inc.
Penguin	Penguin Books, Inc.
Pocket	Pocket Books
Prentice	Prentice-Hall, Inc.
Random	Random House, Inc.
St. Martin's	St. Martin's Press, Inc.
Scott	Scott, Foresman and Co.
Scribner's	Charles Scribner's Sons
Simon	Simon and Schuster, Inc.
U of Chicago P	University of Chicago Press
Viking	The Viking Press, Inc.
Yale UP	Yale University Press

TITLE CENTERED,
ONE-THIRD
DOWN PAGE

Political Overtones in George Orwell's Literature

NAME OF
STUDENT

by
Janice Reed

NAME OF INSTRUCTOR

Professor Maybrie

COURSE

English 101

DATE

3 June 1998

1"

Sample MLA Title Page

TITLE REPEATED

1"

Political Overtones in George Orwell's Literature

1/2"

Reed 1

DOUBLE-SPACED

WRITER'S LAST NAME AND PAGE NUMBER ON EACH PAGE

George Orwell was one of the most outspoken political writers of his time and spent most of his adult life warning of the dangers of totalitarianism and communism and encouraging a more peaceful, socialistic government. In both his personal life and his writing, he makes a strong and convincing case against the language, politics, and methods of repressive political regimes.

WRITER OPENS WITH THESIS

STANDARD PARENTHETICAL CITATION GIVING AUTHOR AND PAGE NUMBER

Orwell began his writing career with pessimism due to disturbing events he encountered throughout his life (Zwerling 37). He was born in Motihari, India in 1903 under the name Eric Arthur Blair. He joined the republican (Loyalist) army and fought in the Spanish Civil War, finishing the war distrustful of autocracies and bureaucratic hypocrisy. After continual political letdowns, Orwell was a perfect candidate to become a socialist convert (Ousby 922-923). Socialism had come to be known as a virtual "safe haven" for oppressed and downtrodden peoples as well as a refuge for those intolerant of the way politics was enforced at that time (Orwell CD-ROM).

Fighting in the Spanish Civil War was a turning point in George Orwell's life and writing style. As he turned to socialism for the answers to the political ills of the day and became involved in the party, his style of writing began to transform. Before the war, he concerned himself with recounting significant events in his life, mostly in the form of essays (Magill 220). After the war, he dedicated his writing to political commentary and to promoting public awareness. In the Preface to <u>Animal Farm</u> he states, "Every line of serious work that I have written since 1936 has been written, directly or indirectly *against* totalitarianism and *for* democratic socialism, as I understand it" (12). Orwell defined socialism as the state of society based on the values of equality, social justice, cooperation, progress, individual freedom and "public ownership" (social or state control over production and distribution). He sought to achieve this ideological state by abolishing capitalism and reducing the importance of social status. Socialists tried to change governments through popular education and alterations in the constitution, leaving violent revolution as the last resort. Although Orwell was a socialist, his aim was not to convert nonsocialists, but rather to reprove lukewarm socialists, encourage democratic socialists, and win back lost socialists from communism (Draper 807).

ONLY THE PAGE NUMBER IS GIVEN WHERE THE SOURCE IS INTRODUCED IN THE TEXT.

1"

(See "Works Cited," page 70)

34C APA documentation

The style of documentation described in the *Publication Manual of the American Psychological Association** uses parenthetical citations in the written material to document all sources of quotations, paraphrased statements, ideas, or other secondary sources. These parenthetical citations refer to a list of *References*, a complete and detailed list of sources at the end of the paper. Typically, in a citation, you use the author's last name (only) in a sentence that introduces the material to be documented, and, immediately following the name, you put the date of publication in parentheses. When the author's name is not mentioned in your text, you include the author's last name followed by a comma and the date of publication in parentheses at the end of the sentence, or, if you have referred to more than one source, the end of the applicable clause. In addition, when you cite a direct quotation, always include page numbers with your citations or in separate parentheses at the conclusion of the quotation and use *p.* or *pp.* with the page numbers. Do not supply page numbers for any other source unless you have a good reason to, such as supplying the page numbers for a passage that might be very difficult to find. For more information about the source, all the reader has to do is find the author's name on the *References* page at the end of the paper. (If two authors have the same last name, use the authors' initials). One last very important point: because APA papers are generally used in the social sciences (a scientific paper explains what has been substantiated by research within a very specific area), the style demands the use of the past tense or present-perfect tense for sources cited:

> Dawson and Meyers (1989) reported no fewer than twelve incidents of Prozac being ineffective after six months of use.

The present tense can be used in the text for generalizations and references to continuing conditions:

> The use of all drugs prescribed to alter behavior continues to require great care and follow through.

For full information about the APA style, consult the official APA manual in your library or bookstore.

EXAMPLES:

Of a citation in the paper:

> Lear (1998) concludes that William Conant was the most authoritative doctor in Merced County, because he had treated all of the residents for many years.

Of an entry in the References list:

Osborne, D., & Gaebler, T. (1998). Reinventing government: How the entrepreneurial spirit is transforming the public sector. New York: NAL-Dutton.

Publication Manual of the American Psychology Association, 4th Edition (Ninth printing, June 1997).

CITING SOURCES WITHIN THE TEXT OF YOUR PAPER

1. Author named in your text

If the author's name appears in your text, cite only the date of the publication in parentheses, right after the author's name.

> Resener (1997) categorizes the homeless according to the reasons for their displacement: the "Seeker," the "Mentally Ill," the "Stranded," and the "Self-inflicted."

2. Author not named in your text

When you do not mention the author in your text, cite his last name, followed by a comma and the year of publication, in parentheses.

> Some major psychologists argue that the emphasis on group therapy and the dynamics of group discussions may dampen full participation by some subjects (Waller, 1991).

3. Using page numbers

When you cite a quotation, you must include page numbers, either in the parentheses with the author and date of publication, or in separate parentheses at the conclusion of the quotation. Use *p.* or *pp.* before the page numbers.

> Boorstein (1996, pp. 38-39) explained that "few researchers really believe that the impact of the new interviewing protocols issued by the Association would have a significant impact on the conclusions of their studies or on the tables compiled at the end of the year."

Holden (1990) reported the following:

> Unfortunately, in the past, the words *retirement home* often brought to mind impersonal, lonely places. However, conditions in retirement can vary, some homes earning awards for excellence in nursing care, and others earning citations for negligence. Regulations regarding nursing homes are becoming stricter than they once were, and it is possible to find retirement conditions that are positive and comfortable (p. 382).

4. Two authors

When a work has two authors, cite both last names each time you refer to their work. Within the parentheses, use an ampersand (&), but if you refer to them in your text, spell out the word *and*.

> Handler and Neeley (1998) felt that, while the study of grammar is interesting and satisfying to teachers, it does not translate to better writing on the part of the students.

> A well-known study reveals that, while the study of grammar is interesting and satisfying to teachers, it does not translate to better writing on the part of the students (Handler & Neeley, 1998).

5. Three to five authors

When you refer to a work that has three to five authors, cite all the names in your first reference to them. In subsequent references, state only the name of the first author followed by *et al*.

Psychiatric researchers have felt that the use of mood-altering drugs usually results in some relief of symptoms, followed by a gradual return to the original behavior (Bonepane, Annaheim, Mathevon, Blanc, & Stantzos-Liard, 1991, p. 302).

However, the one exception to that rule appears to be Prozac (Bonepane, et al., 1991, p. 314).

Bonepane et al. (1993) have promised a possible breakthrough in the mapping of the brain. (Subsequent first citation per paragraph thereafter.)

Bonepane et al. have promised a possible breakthrough in the mapping of the brain. (Omit year from subsequent citations after first citation within a paragraph.)

6. Six or more authors

Use the first author's name and et al. *every* time you cite this source.

Scientists have isolated a gene that appears to govern patience and general self-control (Miller et al., 1993).

Miller et al. (1993) have promised a possible breakthrough in the mapping of the brain. (Subsequent first citation per paragraph thereafter.)

Miller et al. have promised a possible breakthrough in the mapping of the brain. (Omit year from subsequent citations after first citation within a paragraph.)

7. Organization as author

When you cite a longer than practicable organization for the first time, use the full name, followed by an abbreviation in brackets. When you use it in subsequent citations, use the abbreviation only.

First citation: (Los Angeles Pacific Benevolent Society [LABS]), 1992)

Later citation: (LABS, 1992)

8. Author not named

When you cite a work with author unknown, use a shortened version of the work's title (the full title will appear in your references page).

Since the inception of Proposition 13 reforms, enrollment in most two-year schools has dropped considerably (Index to Community Colleges, 1994).

9. Corporate author

When your source is a corporate or government publication written by a group, use the name of the company or organization. Do not use acronyms for first usage (although acronyms may be used in a subsequent reference). In such a case, use the acronym in brackets when you refer to the organization for the first time.

First citation: The most authoritative work, Guidelines (Council for Resource Development [CRD], 1990), mainly outlines grant opportunities in all the governmental organizations.

Later citation: The CRD holds year-crowning conferences in Washington, D.C. at the end of each year.

10. Two or more works in same parentheses

When you list two or more references in a parenthetical citation, arrange them in alphabetical order, separated by semicolons.

Several participants in the research project (Bonilla, 1993; Frachette, 1993; Lowell, 1994) expressed misgivings about the general summary of the project, written by the director after all members of the team had left.

REFERENCE LIST

APA guidelines for preparation of a *Reference* list are clear and direct, and must be followed scrupulously:

- Begin the *References* list on a new page at the end of your paper.

- Use references judiciously and include only the sources that were used in the research and preparation of the paper. (Use *Bibliography* if you are listing works for background or for further reading.)

- Double-space all lines of an entry and between entries. Do not indent the first line of an entry, but indent every line thereafter five spaces (1/2 inch); this is what is known as a "hanging indent," used for student papers and actual journal articles. (If you are writing an article to be submitted to a publisher, you use traditional paragraph indents).

- List all authors last name first, and use only initials for first and middle names. With two or more authors, continue the last-name first listing, separating authors with a comma, and using an ampersand (&) before the last author's name.

- Immediately after the author or authors, place the date of the publication in parentheses, followed by a period. For magazines, use the year, a comma, and the month or day and month. Do not abbreviate.

- List entries in alphabetical order according to the last name of the authors or editors. When the author or editor is not available, alphabetize by the first word of the title other than the articles (*A, An,* or *The*). If your list includes two works by the same author, list the selections by date, the earliest first. If you are including two articles by the same author in the same year, arrange them alphabetically by title.

- Underline or italicize the titles of books, plays, long poems, pamphlets, periodicals, and films as long as they are published as independent, separate works. Do not place the titles of articles in quotation marks; capitalize only the first word of the article, as well as all proper nouns. Capitalize all major words in a periodical title.

- If the title of a book you are citing includes the title of another book, as in <u>A Resource Book for Joseph Conrad's</u> Lord Jim, underline the main title, but do not underline the included title.

- For a book, list the city of publication (and the country or postal abbreviation for the state if the city is unfamiliar), followed by a colon, and the publisher's name, dropping <u>Inc.</u>, <u>Co.</u>, or <u>Publishers</u>, followed by a period.

- If more than one place of publication is given, use the first city only.

- Use the date a work was published, even if it has had several printings. However, if the source is a new or revised edition, give the date of that edition, not the original date of publication.

REFERENCES

A Book by One Author

Wylie, P. (1942). *Generation of vipers.* New York: Holt, Rinehart, and Winston.

Two or More Books by One Author

Grisham, J. (1989). *A time to kill.* New York: Bantam Books.

Grisham, J. (1991). *The firm.* New York: Bantam Books.

Grisham, J. (1992). *The pelican brief.* New York: Doubleday.

A Book by Two or More Authors

Osborne, D., & Gaebler, T. (1992). *Reinventing government: How the entrepreneurial spirit is transforming the public sector.* Reading, PA: Addison.

A Book by an Anonymous Author

The dictionary of psychological expressions. (1968). New York: Macmillan.

A Book with Editors

Bucker, W. E., & Follett, J.C. (Eds.). (1958). *Clinical studies of the Victorian period.* Boston: Houghton Mifflin.

A Work in an Anthology

Huxley, T. H. (1958). Science and culture. In W. E. Buckler (Ed.), *Prose of the Victorian period* (pp. 320-367). Boston: Houghton Mifflin.

Several References to a Textbook, Casebook, or Anthology

First, make an initial reference to the anthology:

Jacobus, L. (Ed.). (1994). *A world of ideas.* Boston: Bedford Books.

Then, make cross-references to the initial reference:

Darwin, C. (1858). *Natural selection.* In Jacobus, pp. 403-415.

Bacon, F. (1620). *The four idols.* In Jacobus, pp. 385-397.

A Work in Several Volumes

Johnson, E. (1952). *Charles Dickens: his tragedy and triumph.* (Vols. 1-2). New York: Simon and Schuster.

A Second or Later Edition

Azar, B. S. (1989). *Understanding and using English grammar.* (2nd ed.). Englewood Cliffs, NJ: Prentice-Hall.

A Book in a Series

Procter, H. D. (Ed.). (1970). Dysfunction in a multi-sibling family: Children in conflict. In H. R. Obrian (Series Ed.) & P. Keller (Vol. Ed.), *Handbook of social interaction: Vol. 3. The active and healthy family* (2nd ed., pp. 1-209). New York: Prentice-Hall.

A Translation

Hsueh-chin, T. (1958). *Dream of the red chamber.* (C. Wang, Trans.). New York: Doubleday.

A Signed Article in a Reference Book

Wiley, B. (1979). Arnold, Matthew. *The new encyclopedia Britannica.* (Vol. 2, pp. 36-40). Chicago: *Encyclopedia Britannica.*

An Unsigned Article in a Reference Book

Nevada. (1989). *The world book encyclopedia.* (Vol. 14, pp. 156-177). Chicago: *World Book.*

An Article in a Journal with Continuous Pagination

Palmer, G. E., Gordon, M. L., & Rostos, P. (1992). Computer applications in the freshman laboratory. *Journal of Chemical Education, 58,* 995-1156.

An Article in a Journal That Paginates Each Issue Separately

Cummins, P., McBride, J. E., Gaye, P., & Soto, M. C. (1988). Mainstreaming children with cognitive disorders. *Psychological Review, 100,* 143-146.

An Article from a Monthly Publication

Williamson, M. & Rist, B. E. (1992, November 22). A return to love. *Cosmopolitan,* 66-68.

A Signed Article from a Daily Newspaper

Burns, J. F. (1993, January 7) . Stranger in a strange land: Muslim in Serb army. *New York Times,* p. A3.

An Unsigned Article from a Daily Newspaper

Nationsbank card features a savings plan. (1993, January 7). *New York Times,* p. C5.

Lectures, Speeches, and Addresses

Bronstein, W. S., (1997, March). *"The growing child-abuse problems among foster children."* Paper presented at the meeting of the American Professional Society on the Abuse of Children, Sante Fe, N. Mex.

A Book by a Corporate Author

American Psychiatric Association. (1994). Compilation of case loads within public hospital mental wards. (3rd ed.). Washington, DC: Author.

} 1"

MEANS JUSTIFY THE ENDS?   1

Do the Means Justify the Ends?   TITLE

Ralph R. Veralli   STUDENT'S NAME

History 20
}   AFFILIATION
Prof. Justin Drinkwater

May 17, 1998   DATE

Title Page, APA

MEANS JUSTIFY THE ENDS?   2

DO THE MEANS JUSTIFY THE ENDS?

Machiavelli (1966) lived in Italy at the time the country was separated into many small provinces ruled by different princes. His own fortune had been affected by the fact that rulers came and went in his province all the time, so he was interested in princes being wise and holding their power firmly (1979, pp. 65-66). <u>The Prince</u>, his most celebrated work, raises many different questions concerning the way a prince should run his state. In the book, his main concern is not the well-being of people, but helping the ruler maintain his power by any means necessary (1966, p. 246). All through his essay, Machiavelli carries the idea that "the ends justify the means." The question of whether this aphorism is true or not has been raised a great many times throughout the history of mankind. Machiavelli's answer is "yes." The prince needs only be con-cerned with his interests and with achieving the results he wants no matter what it takes. If it takes the lives of innocent citizens—fine, but take those lives in such a way that will not make you "hated or despised" (Machiavelli, 1966). He is not concerned with the minority that might suffer because that fact will be overshadowed by the happiness of the majority at having such a good life and such a great prince (Machiavelli, 1979).

Machiavelli cited many examples of leaders achieving great results by being ruthless, ungrateful, cruel, or dishonest. There were many examples after his time as well. Hitler, for instance, used many deceptions to come into power. He did not say anything about exterminating Jewish people or conquering the world. He spoke about restoring the economy and Germany's position in the world (1971). When he did ascend to power, he said things that appealed to the majority and then did not have to care about the minority (Ayer, 1996, p. 328). Few people worried about a few million minorities if all was better economically and Germany

DATES ALONE SUFFICIENT BECAUSE READERS KNOW THE SUBJECT IS MACHIAVELLI

AUTHOR AND DATE GIVEN

AUTHOR, DATE AND PAGE GIVEN

(See "References," page 70)

34D CMS documentation

The fourteenth edition of *The Chicago Manual of Style* (1993) covers two methods of documentation exhaustively; the method discussed in this manual is known as "Chicago style," and has long been used in history as well as other realms of the arts and humanities. Its use of superscripts is somewhat bothersome to writers, but it has some advantages, the main one being that the superscripts hinder and detract less from the text than parenthetical references. In addition to the *Chicago Manual* mentioned above, consult Kate L. Turabian's *A Manual for Writers of Terms Papers, Theses, and Dissertations*, 6th Edition (1996) for further reference.

MARKING IN-TEXT CITATIONS

The Chicago Manual of Style employs traditional superscript arabic numerals or raised arabic numerals within the text (in this fashion[12]) and footnotes placed at the bottoms of pages on which their corresponding superscript numerals appear.

- Sometimes, instructors ask their students to place all notes in an *Endnotes* section at the end of the paper. You should be sure which of the alternatives your instructor wants you to use.

- Sometimes, too, you are instructed to write a separate *Bibliography* page at the end of the paper on which all sources are arranged alphabetically.

- You should number all notes consecutively throughout the paper.

- Place your superscripts slightly above the line (like this [7]) they should occur immediately after quotations or paraphrases (without a space). Do not put the superscript note numbers before periods, parentheses, brackets, or slash marks; the superscript number follows any punctuation except the dash, and it is always put outside a closing parentheses.

- A superscript numeral in your paper means that a quotation, idea, paraphrase, summary, or statistic has been borrowed from a secondary source; to find the author or publishing details for the source, the reader only has to check the footnote with the same number on the same page (or endnote if you list all your notes on a page at the end of your paper) for the information.

- Avoid the overuse of superscripts. When possible, incorporate your information in the explanatory and supporting material of your paper.

EXAMPLES:

Of a superscript numeral in the paper:

> Carl Resener categorizes the homeless according to the reasons for their displacement: the "Seeker," the "Mentally Ill," "the Stranded," and the "Self-inflicted."[2]

Of a footnote or endnote:

> [2]Carl R. Resener, *Crisis in the Streets* (Nashville: Broadman Press, 1988), 66.

CONVENTIONS FOR NOTES

Chicago Manual guidelines for preparation of footnotes or endnotes are clear and direct, and must be followed scrupulously:

- The first time you refer to a citation in the notes, give a complete entry in the correct format for the bibliographical style you are employing in the paper; afterwards, use the last name of the author and a page number (subsequent references should include only enough information to allow the reader to locate the original note or bibliographical entry).

- Begin with the Arabic numeral corresponding to the number of the citation in the text. Follow the number with a period and one space.

- Insert a space between entries. Single space all lines of an entry.

- Indent the first line of an entry five spaces (one-half inch) and place successive lines flush left.

- Each first entry of a book reference should have the following information (choose what is applicable to the book you are citing):

  Complete name of the author in first-name last-name order;

  Title of the book and subtitle, underlined or italicized;

  Name of editor, compiler, or translator, if any, preceded by ed., trans. or comp.;

  Number of name of edition, if different from the first;

  Name of series in which book appears, if any, with volume or number in the series;

  Within parentheses: the city of publication followed by a colon, the publisher's name followed by a comma, and the date of publication;

  The page number(s) on which the cited information can be found, followed by a period.

- In note references, the items above are separated by commas, or, as in the facts of publication (city of publication, publisher's name, and date of publication), parentheses. Do not place a comma just before the opening parenthesis of the publication facts; however, do place a comma just after the closing parenthesis of the publication facts, before the reference to page number(s).

- In general, all items within the notes are separated by one space.

- Underline the titles of books, plays, long poems, pamphlets, periodicals, films as long as they are published as independent, separate works.

- If the title of a book you are citing includes the title of another book, as in A Resource Book for Joseph Conrad's Lord Jim, underline the main title, but do not underline the included title.

- Use quotation marks for articles, shorter titles, song titles, and unpublished works.

- Use the complete names of publishers, but omit the article *The* and the abbreviations *Inc.*, *Ltd.*, and *S.A.* The ampersand may be used in the place of *and* and *Company*, *Brothers* and the like may be abbreviated (*Co.*, *Bros.*) or omitted.

- If more than one place of publication is given, use the first city only. If the city is not widely known, give the state as well, using standard abbreviations (Glenview, Ill.).

- Use the date a work was published, even if it has had several printings. However, if the source is a new or revised edition, give the date of that edition, not the original date of publication.

- When references to the same work follow one another with no intervening references, use Ibid. (abbreviation of Ibidem, "in the same place"). Normally, you simply give the author's last name followed by a comma and the page or pages cited:

    5. Ibid., 28

    6. Meyer, 86

The following examples provide models for first notes:

A Book by One Author

1. Philip Wylie, *Generation of Vipers* (New York: Holt, Rinehart, & Winston, 1942), 104.

Two or More Books by One Author

2. John Grisham, *The Firm* (New York: Bantam, 1991), 78.

3. John Grisham, *A Time to Kill* (New York: Bantam, 1989), 34.

4. John Grisham, *The Pelican Brief* (New York: Doubleday, 1992), 207.

A Book by Two or Three Authors

5. David Osborne and Ted Gaebler, *Reinventing Government: How the Entrepreneurial Spirit Is Transforming the Public Sector* (Reading: Addison, 1992), 366-368.

A Book by Four or More Authors

6. George Ehrenhaft et al., *How to Prepare for the ACT* (New York: Barron's Educational Series, 1991), 67.

Institution or Association as Author

7. American Library Association, Young Adult Services Division, *The Key to English: Figurative Expressions* (New York: Macmillan, 1966), 46.

A Book with an Editor

8. William E. Bucker, ed., *Prose of the Victorian Period* (Boston: Houghton Mifflin, 1958), 55.

A Book with an Author and an Editor

9. Jules Verne, *Voyage from the Earth to the Moon*, ed. A. Boucher (New York: Dodd & Mead, 1956), 222.

A Work in an Anthology

10. Thomas Henry Huxley, "Science and Culture," in *Prose of the Victorian Period*, ed. William E. Buckler (Boston: Houghton Mifflin, 1958), 488.

A Book in a Series

11. Henry D. Piper, ed., *Fitzgerald's The Great Gatsby: The Novel, The Critics, The Background*, Scribner Research Anthologies (New York: Charles Scribners, 1970) , 144.

A Translation

12. Hsueh-chin, Tsao, *Dream of the Red Chamber*, Trans. Chi-Chen Wang (Garden City, N.J.: Doubleday, 1958), 14 .

A Signed Article in a Reference Book

13. *Encyclopedia Britannica*. 15th ed., s.v. Wiley Basil, "Arnold, Matthew."

An Unsigned Article in a Reference Book

14. *The World Book Encyclopedia*, 1989 ed., s.v. "Postal Union, Universal."

An Article in a Journal with Continuous Pagination

15. Glenn E. Palmer, "Computer Applications in the Freshman Laboratory," *Journal of Chemical Education* 58 (1981): 995.

An Article in a Journal That Paginates Each Issue Separately

16. Paul Cummins, "Teaching Modern Poetry," *California English Journal*, 5.2 (1969): 43-46.

An Article from a Monthly Publication

17. Marianne Williamson, "A Return to Love," *Cosmopolitan*, Dec. 1992, 66-68.

A Signed Article from a Daily Newspaper

18. John F. Burns, "Stranger in a Strange Land: Muslim in Serb Army," *New York Times*, 7 Jan 1993, sec 1:A3.

An Unsigned Article from a Daily Newspaper

19. "Nationsbank Card Features a Savings Plan," *New York Times*, 7 Jan 1993, sec. C:5.

Interviews

20. Barbara Miller, interview by author, Los Angeles, 22 October 1992.

ELECTRONIC DOCUMENTS

Electronic media are of two main types: (1) CD-ROMS, disks, or tapes that you physically carry with you and load into your computers; (2) on-line resources such as information you find on the Internet, listserv mail, or e-mail. In both cases you can print out the resource, and document it in the same way as printed material.

The same basic information is required (whatever is available to you):

- author and title of a particular source
- name and description of the source cited, whether CD-ROM, listserv, e-mail, or an on-line source
- publisher or vendor (or both)
- date of publication or access (or both)
- identifying numbers or the pathway needed for retrieval of the material

Material on CD-ROM

21. United States v. Shabani, document no. 93-981. (U.S. Supreme Ct. 1994), reproduced in SIRS Government Reporter CD-ROM [CD-ROM] (Boca Raton, FL: Social Issues Resources Series, 1995).

Material on Disk

22. Joyce McBride, "A Letter to My Mother," (Worcester: Eastgate, 1997), diskette.

Material Accessed via Networks

23. Jonathan King, "Sex, Lies, and the Internet," *Microsoft Internet Magazine*, 2 March 1998 [magazine on-line]; available from http://home. microsoft.com/reading/archives/feature-3-2-98.asp; Internet; accessed 8 June 1998.

24. Ariel Pablos-Mendez et al, "Global Surveillance for Antituberculosis-Drug Resistance," *New England Journal of Medicine* [on-line] 4 June 1998 [journal on-line]; available from http://www. nejm.org/public/1998/0338/0023/1641/1 .htm; Internet; accessed 12 June 1998.

E-Mail and Other Electronic Messages

25. Earl Patterson, "Re: Faulkner Summer Seminar," e-mail to Fred Obrecht, accessed 8 June 1996.

BIBLIOGRAPHY

Bibliographical lists (an alphabetized arrangement of all of your sources) are not always required by instructors. They should not be necessary in a relatively short term paper where the notes are easily accessed, even though they are not in alphabetical order. If they are required, you should follow the MLA guidelines for a list of Works Cited but label your list *Bibliography* (or *Work Cited* or *Sources Consulted*, if one of these titles better describes your list). The *Chicago Manual* method requires you to single-space all entries, with one blank line between entries.

Bibliography

Bucker, William E., ed. *Prose of the Victorian Period.* Boston: Houghton Mifflin, 1958.

Burns, John F. "Stranger in a Strange Land: Muslim in Serb Army." *New York Times*, 7 Jan. 1993, 1:A3.

Cummins, Paul. "Teaching Modern Poetry." *California English Journal*, May 1969.

Ehrenhaft, George, Robert L. Lehrman, Fred Obrecht, and Allan Mundsack. *How to Prepare for the ACT.* 11th ed. New York: Barron's, 1998.

(See "Endnotes" and "Bibliography," page 70)

TRADITIONAL AND POSTAL STATE ABBREVIATIONS

STATE	TRADITIONAL ABBREVIATION (Chicago Manual)	U.S. POSTAL ABBREVIATION MLA and APA
Alabama	Ala.	AL
Alaska	Alaska	AK
Arizona	Ariz.	AZ
Arkansas	Ark.	AR
California	Calif.	CA
Colorado	Colo.	CO
Connecticut	Conn.	CT
Delaware	Del.	DE
District of Columbia	D.C.	DC
Florida	Fla.	FL
Georgia	Ga.	GA
Hawaii	Hawaii	HI
Idaho	Idaho	ID
Illinois	Ill.	IL
Indiana	Ind.	IN
Iowa	Iowa	IA
Kansas	Kans.	KS
Kentucky	Ky.	KY
Louisiana	La.	LA
Maine	Maine	ME
Maryland	Md.	MD
Massachusetts	Mass.	MA
Michigan	Mich.	MI
Minnesota	Minn.	MN
Mississippi	Miss.	MS
Missouri	Mo.	MO
Montana	Mont.	MT
Nebraska	Nebr.	NE
Nevada	Nev.	NV
New Hampshire	N.H.	NH
New Jersey	N.J.	NJ
New Mexico	N.Mex.	NM
New York	N.Y.	NY
North Carolina	N.C.	NC
North Dakota	N.Dak.	ND
Ohio	Ohio	OH
Oklahoma	Okla.	OK
Oregon	Oreg.	OR
Pennsylvania	Pa.	PA
Puerto Rico	P.R.	PR
Rhode Island	R.I.	RI
South Carolina	S.C.	SC
South Dakota	S.Dak.	SD
Tennessee	Tenn.	TN
Texas	Tex.	TX
Utah	Utah	UT
Vermont	Vt.	VT
Virginia	Va.	VA
Washington	Wash.	WA
West Virginia	W.Va.	WV
Wisconsin	Wis.	WI
Wyoming	Wyo.	WY

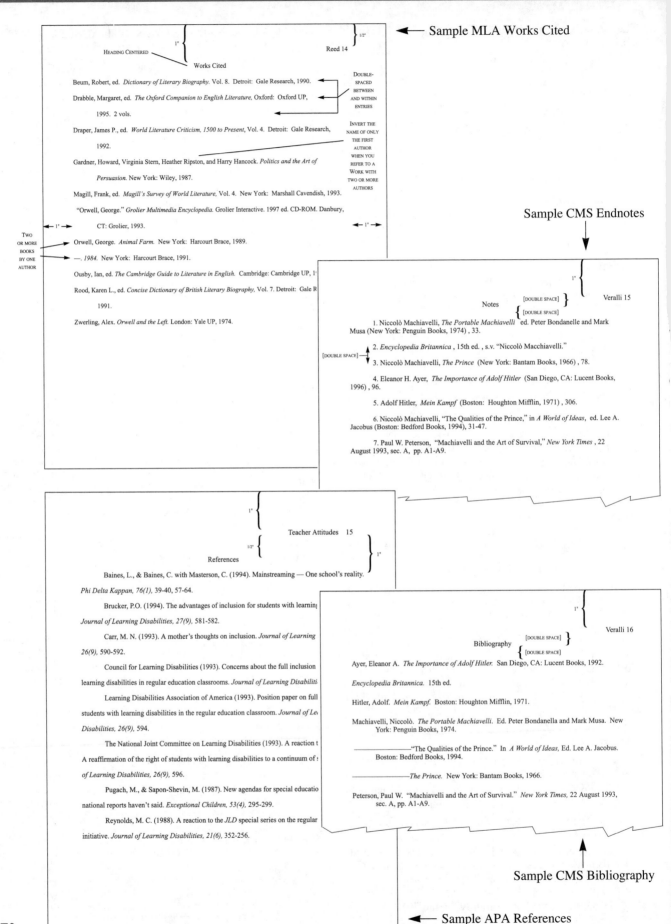

Sample MLA Works Cited

HEADING CENTERED

Reed 14

Works Cited

DOUBLE-SPACED BETWEEN AND WITHIN ENTRIES

Beum, Robert, ed. *Dictionary of Literary Biography.* Vol. 8. Detroit: Gale Research, 1990.

Drabble, Margaret, ed. *The Oxford Companion to English Literature,* Oxford: Oxford UP,

1995. 2 vols.

INVERT THE NAME OF ONLY THE FIRST AUTHOR WHEN YOU REFER TO A WORK WITH TWO OR MORE AUTHORS

Draper, James P., ed. *World Literature Criticism, 1500 to Present,* Vol. 4. Detroit: Gale Research,

1992.

Gardner, Howard, Virginia Stern, Heather Ripston, and Harry Hancock. *Politics and the Art of*

Persuasion. New York: Wiley, 1987.

Magill, Frank, ed. *Magill's Survey of World Literature,* Vol. 4. New York: Marshall Cavendish, 1993.

"Orwell, George." *Grolier Multimedia Encyclopedia.* Grolier Interactive. 1997 ed. CD-ROM. Danbury,

CT: Grolier, 1993.

TWO OR MORE BOOKS BY ONE AUTHOR

Orwell, George. *Animal Farm.* New York: Harcourt Brace, 1989.

—. *1984.* New York: Harcourt Brace, 1991.

Ousby, Ian, ed. *The Cambridge Guide to Literature in English.* Cambridge: Cambridge UP, 1[...]

Rood, Karen L., ed. *Concise Dictionary of British Literary Biography,* Vol. 7. Detroit: Gale R[...]

1991.

Zwerling, Alex. *Orwell and the Left.* London: Yale UP, 1974.

Sample CMS Endnotes

Veralli 15

Notes [DOUBLE SPACE]

[DOUBLE SPACE]

1. Niccolò Machiavelli, *The Portable Machiavelli* ed. Peter Bondanelle and Mark Musa (New York: Penguin Books, 1974) , 33.

2. *Encyclopedia Britannica* , 15th ed. , s.v. "Niccolò Macchiavelli."

3. Niccolò Machiavelli, *The Prince* (New York: Bantam Books, 1966) , 78.

4. Eleanor H. Ayer, *The Importance of Adolf Hitler* (San Diego, CA: Lucent Books, 1996) , 96.

5. Adolf Hitler, *Mein Kampf* (Boston: Houghton Mifflin, 1971) , 306.

6. Niccolò Machiavelli, "The Qualities of the Prince," in *A World of Ideas,* ed. Lee A. Jacobus (Boston: Bedford Books, 1994), 31-47.

7. Paul W. Peterson, "Machiavelli and the Art of Survival," *New York Times* , 22 August 1993, sec. A, pp. A1-A9.

Teacher Attitudes 15

References

Baines, L., & Baines, C. with Masterson, C. (1994). Mainstreaming — One school's reality.

Phi Delta Kappan, 76(1), 39-40, 57-64.

Brucker, P.O. (1994). The advantages of inclusion for students with learning

Journal of Learning Disabilities, 27(9), 581-582.

Carr, M. N. (1993). A mother's thoughts on inclusion. *Journal of Learning*

26(9), 590-592.

Council for Learning Disabilities (1993). Concerns about the full inclusion

learning disabilities in regular education classrooms. *Journal of Learning Disabiliti*

Learning Disabilities Association of America (1993). Position paper on full

students with learning disabilities in the regular education classroom. *Journal of Le*

Disabilities, 26(9), 594.

The National Joint Committee on Learning Disabilities (1993). A reaction t

A reaffirmation of the right of students with learning disabilities to a continuum of s

of Learning Disabilities, 26(9), 596.

Pugach, M., & Sapon-Shevin, M. (1987). New agendas for special educatio

national reports haven't said. *Exceptional Children, 53(4),* 295-299.

Reynolds, M. C. (1988). A reaction to the *JLD* special series on the regular

initiative. *Journal of Learning Disabilities, 21(6),* 352-256.

Veralli 16

Bibliography [DOUBLE SPACE]

[DOUBLE SPACE]

Ayer, Eleanor A. *The Importance of Adolf Hitler.* San Diego, CA: Lucent Books, 1992.

Encyclopedia Britannica. 15th ed.

Hitler, Adolf. *Mein Kampf.* Boston: Houghton Mifflin, 1971.

Machiavelli, Niccolò. *The Portable Machiavelli.* Ed. Peter Bondanella and Mark Musa. New York: Penguin Books, 1974.

————"The Qualities of the Prince." In *A World of Ideas,* Ed. Lee A. Jacobus. Boston: Bedford Books, 1994.

————*The Prince.* New York: Bantam Books, 1966.

Peterson, Paul W. "Machiavelli and the Art of Survival." *New York Times,* 22 August 1993, sec. A, pp. A1-A9.

Sample CMS Bibliography

Sample APA References

35 LITERARY CRITICISM

For those readers who like to discuss books and authors, the term *literary criticism* means the whole body of articles, discussions, interpretations, biographies, and studies that surround major fictional works. Literary criticism can take a lifetime of scholarship and study to master; however, even the beginning student of literature can benefit from looking at the range of perspectives that are available to any reader. Indeed, it is probably the case that the more critical approaches that a reader perceives, the better and more knowledgeable a reader he or she is. It is important to understand that each approach to criticism is seldom used separately, and that the best interpretive essays about literature, while they may favor one, almost always blend several critical approaches.

Literary Schools

1. Moral Criticism
2. Psychological Criticism
3. Sociological Criticism
4. Formal Criticism
5. Archetypal Criticism

1. **Moral criticism** is one of the oldest approaches to literature and art, originating with Plato when he labeled poetry dangerous because it appeals to the emotions rather than the intellect. Plato's opinion was the first expression of concern over the effect of literature on life. Moralist critics throughout the ages have held that what we read is crucial to the quality of our minds and lives, and that all literature should be gauged by its ability to aid and comfort man, and by its success in evoking a higher and more elevated sense of life. Commentaries that are concerned with the effect of literature on life, particularly on the mind and spirits of the reader, are examples of moral literature. An example of a moral critical discussion is Edmund Fuller's 1957 essay "The New Compassion in the American Novel" in which he condemns some contemporary novelists for depicting vicious and criminal behavior without assigning some judgment or blame.

2. Originating with Freud's portrayal of man as a victim of both his own compulsions and the repressive mores of society, **Psychological criticism** delves into three revealing areas: (a) the author's life and times, and the manner in which such biographical information illuminates the work of literature; (b) the characters in the stories, their motivations and behavior; and (c) psychological implications of the creative process itself, possibly with examinations of the creative urge of the artist, and the need for art in society. The chapter about Emily Bronte's *Wuthering Heights* in Somerset Maugham's *The Art of Fiction,* in which he demonstrates the close link between her repressive life and the creation of her novel, is an example of psychological criticism.

3. **Sociological criticism** attempts to place literary works in the broad historical tapestry that constitutes human life on earth. It typically parallels the significant issues and events in the story with others in the past, demonstrating how a literary work acts as a mirror of society and how social forces are an inescapable influence on the artist. Novels about great social upheavals like wars or major migrations are frequently the subject of sociological critical commentaries. Edgar Johnson's critical commentary on the novel *Hard Times* in his biography *Charles Dickens: His Tragedy and Triumph* is an example of sociological criticism. The essay describes Charles Dickens' violent hostility to industrial capitalism and the inhumane spirit of Victorian materialism, particularly as they affected the poor and down-trodden masses.

A contemporary approach to literature that might be considered an offshoot of sociological criticism is **Feminist criticism** which was developed along with movements for women's freedom and equality. Feminist criticism takes on social and cultural conventions which have subjugated women through the ages, such as the patriarchal organization of civilization, and exposes the prejudice that lies behind each.

4. **Formal criticism** places great precedence on reliability of information, focusing on intrinsic meanings within each work of literature, and pointedly avoiding external references such as the biography of the author or contemporary historical events. Formal critics base their analyses only on the works themselves, which they consider objective, reliable sources of information; consequently, their critical essays often emphasize close textual readings and in-depth examinations of structural elements, the study of sentence form, for example, or an analysis of symbolic themes within the novel. An example of a formal critical essay is Erich Auerbach's chapter in *Mimesis,* "Odysseus' Scar," in which he parallels the narrative style of the *Old Testament* with the style of Homer's *The Odyssey,* drawing conclusions about the attitudes and philosophies of both narrative voices.

Somewhat related to formal criticism are the newer **Reader response** approaches to interpretation which discard the concept of a work of literature as a finished statement. These approaches instead view reading as a series of instantaneous responses on the part of the reader as his eyes follow a text on the page of a book. This shift of perspective converts a literary work into an activity that happens in the mind of the reader consisting of different kinds of expectations, that are fulfilled or not fulfilled as he reads, and that are then deferred, changed, modified, and restructured in the flow of the reader's experience. Most reader response critics agree that the experiences created in the mind of the reader are unique; hence, there is no "correct" reading or interpretation of a work, though literary conventions, codes, and rules of language help to structure their reading experience. On the other hand, the reader-response theory known as **Deconstruction** rejects the idea of any structural controls, and views any reading as a series of individual observations which generate many contradictory but never final meanings. Deconstruction scholars study what is there to deconstruct, to learn how meaning is produced, how language works against itself, and how the reader's experience is involved in the generation of meaning.

5. The **Archetypal critical approach** allows the commentator to study literature in its relationship to all humanity, past and present. It was first derived from the anthropological studies of Sir James Frazer, who found startling similarities of language and thought among civilizations separated by centuries and continents. The approach was carried further by psychologist Carl Jung, who developed a theory of the "collective unconscious," the belief that all men preserve a prehistorical knowledge that was once expressed in myths and folk tales. The subject of archetypal critical commentaries are almost always works which have as their premise the existence of a myth or a universal pattern of thought. An example of archetypal criticism is Frederick Hoffman's discussion of William Faulkner's "The Bear," in which he finds references to eternal curses, as well as age-old injunctions on the races to live in peace with their fellow man.

INDEX